ORIGINAL KNOWING

ORIGINAL KNOWING

How Religion, Science, and the Human Mind
Point to the Irreducible Depth of Life

J. Bradley Wigger

CASCADE *Books* • Eugene, Oregon

ORIGINAL KNOWING
How Religion, Science, and the Human Mind Point to the Irreducible Depth of Life

Cascade Books
An Imprint of Wipf and Stock Publishers
199 W. 8th Ave., Suite 3
Eugene, OR 97401

www.wipfandstock.com

ISBN 13: 978-1-61097-608-4

Cataloging-in-Publication data:

Wigger, J. Bradley.

Original knowing : How religion, science, and the human mind point to the irreducible depth of life / J. Bradley Wigger.

xiv + p. 186 ; 23 cm. Includes bibliographical references.

ISBN 13: 978-1-61097-608-4

1. Religion and science. 2. Cognitive science. 3. Knowledge, Theory of. I. Title.

BL240.3 W50 2012

Manufactured in the U.S.A.

To Steve and John

Contents

Acknowledgments ix
Introduction: Wonder xi

PART I *Origins*

1 The Tree of Knowing 3
2 The Great River of Time 10
3 Life Upon Life 20

PART II *Rocks, Roots, and Relationships*

4 Etchings 29
5 The Hatchet 37
6 Promethean Moments 47
7 A Little Speculation 59
8 Monarchs and the Mousterian Mind 68

PART III *Listen Carefully*

9 A Time to Talk 83
10 From Screeches to Speeches:
     How Did Words Come About? 92
11 Rhythm of the Saints 103

PART IV *The Butterfly Effect*

12 Originality, Time, and Education 115
13 Blueberry Picking 124
14 The Age of Religious Knowing 136
15 Primed for More 142
16 In the Beginning 151

Contents

PART V   *Irreducible*

17   The Rivers and Falls of Consciousness   157
18   Stranger Perspectives   164
19   Home   175

Bibliography   181

Acknowledgments

I THANK THE FRIENDS, family, and students who have listened to the ponderings feeding this book. A special thanks to Jane and to all those who let me borrow our conversations. I am grateful to Louisville Presbyterian Theological Seminary, where I work, for the time to write, and to the good folk at Cascade Books, especially Christian Amondson and Chris Spinks, for bringing this book to life.

Introduction

Wonder

THE BOOK YOU HOLD is about knowing—*episteme* from the language of Plato and Aristotle—and the field is called *epistemology*, the study of knowing. Yet Greek names and philosophical categories are not where my thoughts on the subject begin. Instead my mind wanders to a lake in Northwestern Ontario where, growing up, my family would visit summer after summer.

A thousand miles from our home in Southern Illinois, beyond the labyrinthine waters of the Lake of the Woods, on the other side of the Ojibwa territory of Sabaskong Bay, in the middle of a unique and rugged terrain geologists call the Canadian Shield, a dirt road breaks off from the highway and, if the rains have not washed it out, twists and turns its way down to a pond. From that pond flows a creek, and by foot you can follow the water down a steep hillside where it empties into an enormous crystal-clear lake with a small wooden dock that, by day, is perfect for launching a canoe, fishing line, or yourself into the ever-chilly waters. But not at night. At night the best thing to do is to have a seat on the dock's edge and look. Removed from artificial light, and with the sun shaded by the earth itself, the universe sparkles. If you're lucky, not only from the canopy of stars, but from *aurora borealis*, the northern lights, glowing and gliding about the horizon to music you can almost hear.

When I think about knowing, I think about late summer nights on that dock, a pew in the Temple of the Great Dazzling Dome, watching the northern lights.

Knowing—our minds and bodies alike all tangled together like so many vines in a jungle of human awareness. It begins with our bodies, arms stretching to hold and eyes searching to behold a world yielding so much. Textures, noises, smells, warmth, light, shapes, and more flooding the senses directly and immediately whether we can name them, ponder, or even remember them, or not. Our senses lead the way, but it does not take long for words and ideas, thinking and reflecting, to catch on, resulting in new vistas to contemplate, places we have never been, times we can never visit, edges of a universe we can only imagine, or regions of our own minds we can only glimpse indirectly. Feet dangling in the cool water of a Canadian lake, I look to the lights above and wonder why they are, why we are, why there is anything at all.

As a child, I somehow came to believe that the northern lights were created by the sun's rays bouncing off an icy north pole. The explanation seemed good enough, given what I knew at the time of light and dark and reflective surfaces such as the lake itself. Sometime since, I have learned that the phenomenon is actually a result of charged particles from solar winds slipping into the atmosphere through bows in the magnetic field surrounding the earth. I am not sure which explanation is more enchanting. In either case, all this visible beauty derives from unseen forces we can only imagine. So much more is going on, all the time, than our daytime vision can grasp.

My siblings, both brothers, grew up to become scientists—one a geophysicist the other an environmental engineer. I grew up to become a minister, and then a seminary professor who trains ministers. Scientists and religious professionals serve very different roles in society these days, yet at work in us all are the same abilities to sense things visible and ponder things invisible—the sensed and the non-sensed, tangled together in a way that constantly generates questions about who we are and our place in a cosmos that continues to throw on light shows, now, for our own children.

So, as I think about the subject of this book, I have come to consider it less as an academic problem—though there are plenty plaguing the field—I have come to consider the subject of knowing as our way into something more, something at work in religion and science alike; in the words of Abraham Heschel, our way into *radical amazement.*

Connected to, but more than, our ability to think, radical amazement is radical not in the single-minded sense of extreme or all-out, as the word is so often employed today. It is radical in an older sense of the word—having to do with origins, digging down into deep soil to find the roots, in this case perhaps the roots of knowing, the roots of wonder, or maybe the wondrous roots of life itself. "Radical amazement," says Heschel, "refers to all of reality; not only to what we see, but also to the very act of seeing as well as to our own selves, to the selves that see and are amazed at their ability to see."[1] When I consider the subject of knowing I think of the heavens and the earth and the roots of life itself and wonder how, amazed, we can be mindful of them.

∞

Truth be told, this radical ability to be amazed at our own ability to see is odd. Somewhere along the line the human mind took a strange turn. We developed the capacity to turn seeing upon itself, to reflect upon reflection. We are able to ask big questions not only of the universe and our place in it, but we can ask about the very ability to ask big questions. What kind of mind is it after all that even attempts to grasp heaven and earth and the invisible powers flinging galaxies into being? What kind of knowing dares to comprehend a past before anyone existed? What kind of vision sees beneath the surface of things or dreams of understanding the mind itself? Why do we wonder anything at all? The human mind—not only strange, but dizzying.

The fact is our ability to know anything at all has a deep history. Our capacity for wonder has a story, one full of characters and creatures and a profound—even sacred—sense that there is more to life than our eyes can capture. To my biblically formed imagination the tale begins with creation and the One breathing out the heavens and the earth and everything in them. In this story, our strange twist in knowing could be traced to the first couple and a certain tree of knowledge. Before the geological sciences began stretching our sense of creation's timeline or before the biological sciences began disturbing our sense of origins, tracing our roots or the origins of knowing was a much simpler enterprise, an epistemological Eden. But now, having eaten from the tree of evolutionary knowledge, we face the naked realization that knowing itself has taken an immense journey.

The result is a weird new breed of questions as we discover more and more about our prehistoric past—questions about the mind. While fossil digs and carbon dating tell a remarkable story about the bones and the times of our ancient ancestors, we cannot help but wonder what they knew. What did they think about? Could they imagine? How intelligent were they? Who developed language and when? Who were the first religious creatures? In other words, if talking, self-consciousness, or religious awareness did not

1. Heschel, *Man Not Alone*, 11–13.

spring from the first biblical couple, then from whom? When? Who are the prehistorical equivalents? Were Neanderthals self-aware? Could Ardi talk? Did Lucy know God? To the minister in me, these are uncomfortable questions, in part because the answers are not going to be found in the texts I have been trained to study—not directly anyway. But to the human being in me, curious about the mind itself, the questions are not going away. And from my brothers, and the world of knowledge behind them, I have come to appreciate different kinds of texts—rocks and dirt and fossils that testify to other kinds of unseen powers and a depth to life, a depth to ourselves, that words cannot contain. This book explores such depth.

So, from hunting fossils along the Mississippi to campfire conversations over beer, this book digs for the roots of the human mind. Through dreams and rivers, with butterfly migrations and gods, clues are sought to better understand this odd creature who walks and worships and ponders the origins of its own existence. What kind of knowing is uniquely human and what is not? When do babies point and why does it matter? What does throwing a Frisbee reveal about our distant ancestors? Is language the key to our minds as many believe? Or perhaps the heart of knowing rests in something more basic—in a smile—and the powerful social abilities at work allowing us to sense more than the eye can see. Exploring such questions, I take contemporary science as seriously as religious tradition for insight and inspiration alike. From ancient creation stories and how children think about God to archeological digs and the most recent studies in animal behavior, I believe religion and science alike point to an irreducible depth to life—to our own lives—a depth that our minds help us glimpse if only through a glass darkly.

∞

When the sun settles down for the evening and universe begins to grow before our very eyes with its moon and stars and sparkling wonders, when we be begin to appreciate how much more there is and imagine how much greater still the cosmos must be, then, perhaps only then, can we sense how puny our knowledge is, as limited as a child looking out from a dock in the Ontario wilderness. Such a vision should bewilder the beholder, but it never does. An awareness instead dances along the horizon of knowing, hinting that we too are part of the music.

PART I

ORIGINS

SEVERAL YEARS AGO I set about reading everything I could on the subject of consciousness, exploring the possibility of writing about the subject myself. During that period—well before writing the words here—I had a dream. In the dream I see myself standing between the bookcase of our living room and my favorite chair for writing. I am holding a book I had penned. The title: *Original Knowing*.

I see the book in my hands.

∞

Strange things happen when the human mind becomes both the subject and object of its own thinking—something like seeing yourself in a dream, like holding a book of your own thoughts in your hands. Yet this is where we all find ourselves as knowers, where the journey begins: with a mind that dreams and reflects upon itself, one full of images, memories, and more eddying about in some intangible space like the currents of a great river. Here is where human knowers are. How knowers know themselves.

Yet the same mind, awake and sensing, streams about a touchable world filled with rivers and books and favorite chairs and people who dream and so much more. A world within and a world without—knowing encompasses both realms and the mind is reducible to neither. At best we stand on a threshold looking both ways.

How did we get here? How did *Homo sapiens*, knowing humans, arrive at such a threshold? The book in your hands explores this journey, beginning within, then moving without—through time—and back again.

1

The Tree of Knowing

"ORIGINAL KNOWING—ORIGINAL SIN," I said to Jane after describing the dream to her. We have been married long enough she could tell where I was headed and without words she offered a cup of coffee, suggesting by the gesture it was too early for such gloomy theological talk. But it didn't work. "After all," I justified, "it was eating from the tree of *knowing* that led to all their trouble." In saying this I was connecting the title of this dream-book to the old theological idea rooted in the story of Adam and Eve.

In the book of Genesis, God says: "You may freely eat of every tree of the garden; but of the tree of the knowledge of good and evil you shall not eat, for in the day that you eat of it you shall die" (2:16b–17). Tempted by the crafty serpent "to be like God," Adam and Eve indeed eat the fruit, and like a bad dream they realize they are naked and in trouble. Exiled from Eden, cursed to a life of toil and pain, they do eventually die. Original knowing—original sin: to my Calvinist imagination these "originals" are as intertwined as a snake in a tree limb and seem to have something to do with original death as well.

"Too much consciousness," Jane said. And her words triggered another connection for me.

"Origins of consciousness," I thought to myself. It was Julian Jaynes who first stirred my curiosity about the subject over two decades ago. Specifically it was his breathtaking book with the in-your-face title, *The Origins of Consciousness in the Breakdown of the Bicameral Mind*. I remembered that, for Jaynes, the tree of knowledge was a story about the emergence of consciousness—a sense of *I*—in humanity and a corresponding loss of God. For Jaynes, before self-consciousness, people were guided by the

Gods—voices and visions that manifested whenever a critical choice was faced. When Aphrodite appeared to Odysseus or when the prophet Amos heard "the voice of the Lord" these were no mere literary conventions, but vestiges of an earlier era. (For Jaynes, a religious skeptic, this was simply one side of the brain talking to the other, thus the "bi-cameral" mind, just as people with schizophrenia or under severe stress might experience today.) Now, having eaten the fruit of consciousness, the *I* emerges, replaces the voice of God, and paradise is lost.

A radical theory to be sure, but it awakened my own interests in the subject and the way theories of consciousness could have profound implications for religion, if not my dream world as Jane suggested.

"What if," Jane said, "you did write a book and called it *Original Knowing*? A dream book becomes a real book—"

"—in which I write about the dream book," I added, tickled by the idea; and an image popped into my mind. It was the drawing by M. C. Escher called *Drawing Hands*, a visual paradox as so many of his popular works are. This one depicts two hands drawing each other into being. Each hand—one left and one right—is heavily shadowed and detailed, suggesting depth and realism; yet the arms and cuffs are composed of a few simple lines, contrasting the drawer from the drawn.[1]

Knowing Squared

A *Strange Loop*—that is what Douglas Hofstadter would call the Escher image, if not the dream-book-to-book relationship. Thirty years ago the cognitive scientist wrote his Pulitzer Prize–winning masterpiece, *Gödel, Escher, Bach: An Eternal Golden Braid*, examining the paradoxes not only in *Drawing Hands* but in so many of Escher's works. Monks ascend and descend stairs only to end up where they began. A stream of water flows and falls, makes turns, streams along more, only to wind up at the top of the falls again. Escher's hand holds a ball that in turn reflects the image of Escher holding the ball. The artist created a softly surreal world with a loopy logic. As Hofstadter puts it, "despite one's sense of departing ever further from one's origin, one winds up, to one's shock, exactly where one

---

1. To view the work, see M.C. Escher: The Official Website, "Picture Gallery, 'Back in Holland 1941–1954.'"

had started out."[2] Think of Dorothy waking up at the conclusion of *The Wizard of Oz*.

Between *Gödel, Escher, Bach* and his more recent *I Am a Strange Loop*, Hofstadter shares a lifetime of attending to such paradoxes not only in visual art but in music, mathematics, logic, computer science, grammar, and in artificial intelligence as well. He also looks to more prosaic phenomena such as the infinite loop of reflections resulting from two mirrors facing each other or from a video camera pointed at its own monitor. Many of these, like Escher drawings, are highly entertaining, but that is not the ultimate point for Hofstadter. In the last analysis the strange loop is the "crux of consciousness," key to our sense of self, to our own ideas about who we are, crucial to the originality and creativity of human knowing.[3]

If correct, our originality as knowers has something to do with a recursive logic that ties together destinations with origins, linking the beginning with the end and back to the beginning again in an eternal braid. If I enter Escher's *Drawing Hands* from the right-hand perspective, it is clear I am drawing the left hand. But the more I look, the more I realize that I—the right hand—am the one being drawn. Each hand becomes subject and each hand an object. Each hand is the artist and each hand is the art. Or consider Hofstadter's sentence: "*This analogy is like lifting yourself up by your own bootstraps.*"[4] By using the word "this," the sentence doubles back on itself—something sentences do not ordinarily do. "This analogy" is the subject and then becomes the object of its own description.

So, imagine now that these are not sentences and images double-backing on themselves with these loopy, subject-object, first-person–third-person perspectives. Imagine they are people. "The self comes into being," says Hofstadter, "at the moment it has the power to reflect itself."[5] The self, that is, one's sense of one's own being, the sense of *I* or *me*, is very much like a hand drawing a hand drawing itself. "I" am something like a sentence writing itself. Human consciousness is something like the ruby slippers that

---

2. Hofstadter, *Strange Loop*, 102. I am grateful to the late James E. Loder for introducing me to Hofstadter's work in a PhD seminar long ago. See his use of the strange loop in Loder and Neidhardt, *Knight's Move*.

3. Hofstadter, *GEB*, 709.

4. Hofstadter, *Strange Loop*, 62.

5. Hofstadter, *GEB*, 709

take the dreamer home to herself. It is why, in the end, Hofstadter entitles his summary book on the subject, *I Am a Strange Loop*.[6]

In childhood, this power, this sense of self—what Jaynes meant by *consciousness*—typically emerges during the second year of life.[7] Jean Piaget would call it the birth of the symbolic function—that is, a child can symbolically represent herself to herself. Erik Erikson would call it autonomy—she could use this reflective ability to imagine herself doing this or doing that, generating choice. Howard Gardner sees here the origins of an intrapersonal intelligence—knowing oneself and an interior world as distinct from others. And there are many more theories that describe how the sense of self emerges.[8]

Douglas Hofstadter sees a strange loop—thought processes that refer back to the origins of these processes in an endless loop. There is something about human knowing that not only allows us to be the source of thought, but also the object, an *I* than can refer back to a *me*, opening our eyes in a strange loop of self-referential awareness—a kind of awareness squared. Yet the ability may be at work in all kinds of knowing, not only in self-knowledge, but cascading through math and music, as well as language and art, perhaps even driving their development in the first place. As a student of Piaget, Annette Karmiloff-Smith discovered in her own studies of cognitive development: "Children are not satisfied with success in learning to talk or to solve problems; they want to understand *how* they do these things."[9]

This book represents a kind of strange loop. Knowing reaches back upon itself in order to know more fully its own ability to know, how we have come to do these things. Knowing squared.

Temptations

Sitting in my favorite chair with another cup of coffee and a memorable dream, I reflected more upon reflection itself, upon loops and logic and

6. Hofstadter clarifies that technically he should have called it *"I" Am a Strange Loop* (*Strange Loop*, xv).

7. For Jaynes, people were certainly aware before consciousness, just as a baby is—sensing and engaging the world around them—but they were not aware of their own awareness. See Jaynes, *Origins*, ch. 1.

8. Piaget and Inhelder, *Psychology*, ch. 3; Erikson, *Childhood*, ch. 7; Gardner, *Frames*, ch. 10. For an illustration of this moment in cognitive development with my own child, see Wigger, *Texture*, 106.

9. Karmiloff-Smith, *Beyond Modularity*, 17; emphasis mine.

the way children come to their own self-awareness. "Original knowing—original sin" now seemed thin, reducing the wild metaphorical fullness of a dream into a neat theological doctrine.

What a fascinating breed we are after all, creatures who can think about their own thinking. What kind of mind is it that can ask questions about an invisible past, that dreams and writes, that can draw and make music, that can see analogies, generate metaphors, or tells stories of its own fall into naked self-awareness? Originals to be sure. The mind of humanity dazzles.

Yet here, in our very greatness as creatures, in our originality, may be the greatest of temptations.

Beneath a literal reading of the Genesis tale of temptation rests a compelling set of analogies and metaphors telling us something about who we are and even warning us of the dangers of eating from the "know-it-all tree," as Anne Ulanov calls it.[10] The *I* is a powerful reality, loaded with possibilities for good and for evil, able to reflect upon its naked place in the world, including the death of the *I* itself. Such mortal knowing may even lure us into the false security that we can know like God—infinitely—that our knowledge is the beginning and the end of the matter, a complete system in a fixed, unchanging world. But to buy this illusion is to twist reality, is to reduce life into our ideas of it, which is something like circling around in an Escher drawing, endlessly, with no way out. The temptation is to take our own knowledge too literally, if not Eden itself, and hide there forever.

Most dangerously, the same cognitive abilities that allow us to think and create and imagine in such grand and original ways tempt us into an exalted view of ourselves as creatures, as if we stand on the highest peak in the world for the rest of creation to behold. The very fruits of our minds and hands, which are indeed dazzling compared to other species, frankly, tempt us to puff our chests in conquering creaturely narcissism, alienating us, as if eating from the tree of knowledge leads not to self-conscious humility but to a hunger for more. Our minds, caught in such a loop, exaggerate our originality at the expense of the rest of creation, seducing us into believing the world has been made for us and our disposable pleasures.

No wonder God tried to keep the first couple away.

10. Ulanov, "Consciousness," 246.

∞

"Take a walk?" Jane asked.

"Yeah," I answered. I needed one.

An Invitation

"True knowing," as theologian Jürgen Moltmann describes it, "does not desire to dominate what is known in order to possess it. It wants to arrive at community with the object of its knowledge."[11]

In strange loops, up is down and down is up, and hands draw themselves into being. The staircase takes us up and up into the heights of human knowing with its dazzling originality but dangerous temptations, until we eventually find ourselves back down again, down in the genesis of knowing itself, its origins in some deep beginning a long time ago.

So, in what may be one of the strangest loops of all, our best hope at true knowing may be to use our originality to explore our common origins with all creation, to employ our insight to see deep into the ties that together bind the cosmos. The mind that can ask self-referencing questions about itself can also ask self-referencing questions on behalf of all earth's creatures, if not the universe itself. Not only "Where do I come from?" but "Where do we all come from?"

One hand draws—our knowing sets humanity *apart from* other creatures. The other hand draws—our knowing recognizes humanity as *a part of* creation. We share a family story with all creatures, with the heavens and earth even, in the larger "community of creation" as Moltmann calls it.[12] And perhaps, if we listen carefully, humbly, we can find ourselves, like Dorothy, waking up at home among loved ones, grateful.

Over time, with ongoing reflections, conversations, study, walks, and writing itself, I have begun to see more in my dream than a potential title or book, more than a religious doctrine or strange loop even, more than any one particular idea or interpretation. What began as a fascination with human knowing has remained, but has twisted back around to include more—a wider, if not deeper, community. I have come to see the dream muse issuing an invitation to explore the origins of original knowing in the community of creation.

11. Moltmann, *God in Creation*, 69.

12. Ibid., 70.

So the next chapter gets up out of the chair and takes a walk. To do so is to double our thoughts and dreams back around to beginnings, to home, considering not so much what may be going on inside our minds, but for a moment, to consider what our minds are inside of, where they come from, and when.

2

The Great River of Time

GROWING UP ALONG THE Mississippi—the *Great River* as the Ojibwa called it—my brothers and I often hiked the limestone bluffs towering alongside the waters. Gaining a hundred or more feet over the river's banks not only offered a grand view of the territory, but would inevitably cause time to expand as we considered how long it must have taken the waters to carve out such tall platforms. Hundreds of years, we told ourselves, thousands even. It was an unimaginable quantity of time to consider, but we would try.

The path toward origins inevitably leads through time. It is, as natural scientist Loren Eiseley wrote over a half-century ago, an *Immense Journey*.[1] From either scientific or religious points of view, time expands as our imaginations scale the limestone to take in the territory—from the origins of ourselves as human beings, if not all creatures, to the origins of planets and stars and all there is. Even so, even with this much in common, the difference between the bluffs of time that scientists and theologians scale dizzies me, and at no time have I felt this disparity more than a day with my nephew a few years ago, back home in Southern Illinois.

∞

It was the Friday after Thanksgiving and while the whole world seemed to be out shopping, Patrick, four years old at the time, had another idea, one prompted by his geologist parents. He approached my teenagers and me with a question.

"Do you guys want to go hunt for trilobites?"

---

1. Eiseley, *Immense Journey*.

"What?" my daughter Cora, the child of ministers, asked, assuming that Patrick was mispronouncing something. "What was that Patrick?"

"Do you want to go hunt for trilobites?" This time clearly pronouncing the mystery word: "try—low—bites."

"Uh, sure Patrick," my son David answered, "but what's a trilobite?"

As we gathered our coats, my brother Steve explained to us. "They're some of the oldest critters on earth and you can find their fossils in the limestone along the bluffs."

"Cool, so how old are they?"

"Oh, around here, 500 million or so."

"*Years?*" I questioned, "half a billion *years?*"

"Well, they're Cambrian, so yeah, somewhere in the 500 range give or take 50 million years."

Even as I struggled to get my mind around such an age, I could also feel my own sense of time awakening to possibilities. As we headed down the Great River Road toward the point where the Mississippi and Illinois waters meet, I remembered a scene from Norman Maclean's *A River Runs Through It*, coming, as many poignant moments in that book do, when Maclean and his Presbyterian minister father are out fishing.

The story is set in the early 20th century, when the world was only beginning to reckon with how old it might really be, and Maclean's father notices how some of the river's rocks have raindrops fossilized in them. "His imagination," Maclean writes, "was always stirred by the thought that he was standing in ancient rain spattering on mud before it became rocks."

"Nearly a billion years ago," Maclean suggests, reading his father's thoughts. "Nearly *half* a billion years ago," his father responds. As the younger Maclean reports, it was "his contribution to reconciling science and religion. He hurried on, not wishing to waste any part of old age in debate, except over fishing."[2]

So with Patrick leading the way, we spent a couple of relaxed hours scouting about the bluffs and caves of Southern Illinois' river valley hunting for signs of some of its first multi-celled inhabitants and thinking about time from the perspective of rivers and rocks and old critters whose age could be off by 50 million years and not matter much. If theologians allowed that much slippage, even the tiniest fraction of it, I found myself calculating, it could be the difference between Stone Age burials and Thomas Aquinas. By the geological clock, humanity is just a tick between ice ages.

2. Maclean, *River*, 92.

As we were poking around a wall of rock that appeared promising to the geologists' eyes, I asked no one in particular, "So who or what will be hunting our fossils a half a billion years from now?" Nobody answered.

"Here's one," Ann, Patrick's mother, announced, "part of one anyway." And we all gathered around a sharp break in the bluff wall where we could see evidence of a trilobite—half of one—a primordial bug older than my mind wanted to grasp.

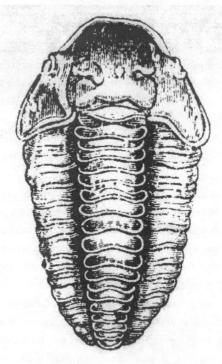

Grasping Time

Somewhere along the line our ancestors crossed a threshold and became, as Eiseley puts it, "a dream animal," creatures no longer locked into an eternal present and ones that, for better or worse, could imagine the past and future.[3] Time, knowing, and origins have been intertwined ever since. Not only *who* do we come from? Or *where?* But *when?* When was the beginning? When is the end? When did our ancestors live? When did people begin to think about beginnings and ends and time itself?

3. Eiseley, *Immense Journey*, 120.

On this side of that threshold, Jean Piaget, the great investigator of young minds, wrote a whole book on the subject, that is, how children develop a sense of chronology. Piaget was prompted by conversations with and questions raised by Albert Einstein, who himself wondered about the origins of our understanding of time. Piaget, in *The Child's Conception of Time*, reminds us of something that every parent knows: to young children time is quite a fluid concept. Their notion of *after* may come before *before* one moment, then after the next. Bigger things are older, shorter people are younger, and yesterday could have been weeks ago, or hours. The young child's sense of order in time is weak. For example, Piaget poured liquid from one jar to another and then asked children to retrace the sequence they observed. Even with pictures to help, most young children had difficulty doing so.[4] Though I did not, had I asked the four-year-old Patrick the question, "Who is older: the trilobite or Uncle Brad?" he might well have said "Uncle Brad." I'm bigger than a trilobite after all, and he's known me all his life (versus the trilobite we just found). Or maybe the trilobite is older because it's part of a huge bluff.

The concept of time, as adults know it, is so difficult for young children because, in Piaget's words, "Grasping time is tantamount to freeing oneself from the present, to transcending space by a mobile effort."[5] And a lot depends upon this mobile effort, our very identities even, that story-like quality to our lives that rivets a sense of past, present, and future together in our dream animal imaginations.

For Piaget, always the logician, that effort is a certain kind of logical ability, one built up through ongoing, bodily, "sensorimotor" experiences that enable a child first of all to recognize the way one thing happens after another in sequences. But that is not enough. The child also must imagine these sequences, in some sort of mental space, and then be able to retrace these in either direction. Piaget calls the ability "reversible operations," which is to say reversible logic or logic that can flexibly reverse the order of a sequence.

So when it comes to time, to perform such an operation is quite a feat when you think about it. A child has to be able to separate the inner, psychological, subjective sense of duration in the present—the feeling that we all still have regarding whether an event goes quickly or takes forever—from the more abstract notion that all sequences and durations can

4. Piaget, *Time*, ch. 1.
5. Ibid., 259.

be divvied up into equal parts and measured by how many of those parts it takes to correspond to an event. The child has to be able to count, then to imagine those numbers along something like a number line in their minds. Then, mentally, they have to compare that number line to an event—one remembered in the past or one anticipated in the future. These two very different kinds of mental frames of reference have to blend together to generate what Piaget calls "rational time."

It is a miracle anyone ever learns to tell time.

Sequences

When I saw the trilobite fossil up close, touching it, I began to feel as if I were learning to tell time all over again. A sense of the ages opened; deep time, as some call it, was becoming more real. Pondering how long it took the river to cut away the bluffs was one thing, but now, with a trilobite resting under a hundred or more feet of limestone, I began to wonder how long it must have taken for the rock above it to form in the first place.

"What is limestone, exactly?" I asked the geologists, easing into my question.

"Sedimentary rock," one of them answered, "mostly calcium carbonate—shells and bones from sea life."

"Hmm." I thought about that for a moment. "*Sea* life?" We were a thousand miles away from an ocean.

"Yeah, once upon a time this was all under water—a tropical ocean—down near the equator in fact, before the continents drifted," my brother offered.

I tried to get my head around the fact that Southern Illinois was once thousands of miles somewhere else, and under an ocean. Then my real question came out. "So how long does it take for bones and shells to become rock?"

"Oh, I think we normally calculate about six thousand years per inch of limestone."

"One inch," I silently realized, "the universe must only be one inch deep."

∞

For those who want to take the Genesis account of creation as a literal time-table, not only was the universe created in six days, but by counting the sequences of generations—all those *begats* in the Bible—you can determine how old creation is. So-called young earth creationism traces the origin of our universe to just over six thousand years ago, depending upon whose accounting you believe and how you interpret biblical words like *generation*. One common dating is 4004 BC, derived by the 17th-century Anglican archbishop James Ussher. Specifically, day one of creation was Sunday, October 23, 4004 BC.

To the current scientific mind that appreciates the deep time of geological ages, Ussher's dating may sound flat out silly, but the truth is that before the emergence of anything like the field of geology or the theory of evolution, the biblically informed imagination had little reason to question such a recent dating of the universe. In fact, Ussher's accounting was in the same ballpark as other notable minds such as Johannes Kepler and Isaac Newton. Nonetheless, about the same time Ussher was establishing his time frame by sequencing the generations of the Bible, the scientist and eventual Catholic bishop Nicolaus Steno was establishing sequences of a different nature, ones that would open up new ways of looking at the earth, creation, and even time itself.

Steno is considered one of the principle founders of geology, and in his own time he was trying to address a fundamental puzzle generated by the Genesis account of creation. As Alan Cutler explains in his wonderful book about the bishop, *The Seashell on the Mountaintop*, the baffling question was: "Why are seashells often found far away from the sea, sometimes embedded in solid rock at the tops of mountains?"[6]

Such shells and other creature fossils (like trilobites) had been known for centuries, if not longer, discovered when stone was quarried for buildings and roads or mined for precious metals. The story of the flood might explain why these fossils were far away (presumably carried by the flood waters immersing the entire earth), but why were such creatures and shells *in* the rock. Genesis is very clear: the seas and the dry land appear on day three of creation; sea creatures and birds on day five; creeping things and land animals on day six. And, according to the Bible, all of this occurred centuries before the flood anyway, since, as Genesis says, Noah was six

6. Cutler, *Seashell*, 8.

hundred years old when the flood came. So how could any creature have ended up deep inside the solid earth that was created so much earlier in time?

When Nicolaus Steno took up these puzzles, he turned to a different text than the Bible for clues and insight, that is, the earth itself. Beneath the question of how seashells could be found inside of solid rock was a more fundamental question: How could any solid body wind up inside another? Given what was known of rocks and shells and the earth itself, how could this happen?

The key, Steno discovered, was water. As he observed how water could carry and deposit sediments in rivers and streams, for example, he realized how these sediments could have, over time, layered themselves over and around ancient creatures to create their fossilized impressions (now geologists call this the "principle of superposition"). In addition, the same process of sedimentation could account for the layers and strata of rock that could be seen on mountainsides, outcroppings, or in quarries.

It was a breakthrough. Like a child learning to tell time, sedimentation allowed Steno to recognize a firm sequence of events happening in the rocks—a sequence we can retrace backward and forward. The great breakthrough, as Cutler explains, was understanding that "layers of bedrock contained a narrative, that it made sense to speak of one rock being 'older' than another." [7] The earth was telling a story.

Why was it such a breakthrough? To the biblically informed mind of the era, the notion that the ground—the dry land of day three—has a story, a timeline within itself, is not so obvious if you believe it all came about in one day. To imagine the rocky earth as having its own narrative was anything but clear. As Cutler puts it, "Scientific geology began with the 'which came first' question, rather than 'how long ago.'" [8] The *how long ago* question would be addressed later, in the centuries to come, but Bishop Steno opened the door to something new, a new way of reading the text of the earth, a new way of knowing about events and places and creatures long forgotten, if in fact they were ever known by human minds at all.

7. Ibid., 110.

8. Ibid., 113. Steno himself tried to reconcile the Genesis account with his newly established geological principles, but the genie was out of the bottle. Other scientists, who did not care whether Genesis was historically accurate or not, ran with the ideas and soon made it difficult to take the "days" of creation literally. By the early nineteenth century, as Cutler (198) points out, Pope Pius VII declared that the "days" of creation did not have to be taken literally.

The visible rocks, Steno discovered, tell an invisible story. Time, know-ing, and origins have been intertwined ever since. To cross the dreamy threshold into deep time is to open our imaginations to deep stories.

Half a Billion

As a result of Bishop Steno's work, if you ask my geophysicist brother, Steve, about the timeline for creation, instead of a six-day, six-thousand-year-old universe, he will tell you the cosmos is about 14 billion years old, while NASA—to be precise—will tell you 13.73 +/- 0.13 billion years.[9] "Soon" afterwards—just 300 million years later—stars and galaxies began to form, but it would take over nine billion more for our own sun and earth to emerge. While the earth is somewhere between 4.6 and 4.7 billion years old, it took another billion years yet for the planet to cool enough to be-come the kind of place we think of now, relatively stable with a solid crust.

Six thousand years or 14 billion? An inch deep or a little more? In retrospect, a Presbyterian minister of the early 20th century landing on "half a billion" was quite an intellectual feat if not a leap of faith. When it comes to time, even those of us who are open to science and religion alike often find ourselves operating with a kind of truce between them, basically doing a version of Rev. Maclean's "half a billion." Not that we really believe the universe is only a half billion years old; we have no idea what it would really mean to reconcile such different time frames, let alone the world-views behind them. What's a trilobite-hunting believer to do, especially in the wake of such fierce public debates?

On the one hand there are those who fear that if the Bible's histori-cal accuracy is questioned, there begins a slippery slope to atheism. This kind of hard-boiled literalism risks missing the softer forms of knowledge, insight, or wisdom that may be best expressed through myth and story, through song and poetry, or through parable and metaphor for example—all for the prize of historical accuracy. On the other hand, many scientifi-cally minded folk dismiss religion for exactly the same reason. The Bible is either historically accurate or it is not. So if it is not, the logic goes, then the Scriptures are wrong, and there is no reason to believe in God. The truth is that scientific atheism and fundamentalist creationism often think in similar ways on this issue, as if they were two hands drawing each other into existence. The issue of time, in such an atmosphere, is so heavy with

9. According to NASA, "Universe 101."

significance, overloaded, as it must bear the weight of God's very existence on its shoulders.

Wondering how earlier theologians approached the Genesis story of creation, I asked my friend and colleague, Kathryn Johnson, an early church historian, about it. Surely, before Darwin, before geology, the early church took the seven-day approach literally. She gave me several good sources, including references from Philo and Augustine, but the best was from the third-century theologian Origen, who takes a careful look at what Genesis says about the fourth day of creation. Genesis says of the fourth day, "God made the two great lights—the greater light to rule the day and the lesser light to rule the night—and the stars" (1:16).

About this line Origen remarks, "What person of intelligence, I ask, will the account seem logically consistent to that says there was a 'first day' and a 'second' and 'third,' in which also 'evening' and 'morning' are named, without a sun, without a moon, and without stars, and even in the case of the first day without a heaven?"[10] In other words, how can we interpret "days" literally if the sun had not even been created yet? The sun and moon—those great timepieces for humanity—are not themselves created until the fourth so-called day. The Genesis passage itself resists such a singular reading. "In general," Kathryn summarized for me, "chronology is not a big interest; they are more concerned to defend the *goodness* of creation."

The more I have reflected upon her comment, the more sense it has made, especially when considering how often the word "good," *tov* in Hebrew, occurs in the creation story—seven times in the first chapter of Genesis. Again and again, with the days of creation, "God saw that it was good," culminating with a declaration at the end of the chapter, "and behold, it was very good."

∞

Creationist or not, getting our minds around the idea of a cosmos nearly 14 billion years old is no easy task. And in fairness to us all, consider the fact that it has only been in the past couple of centuries that anybody has had a clue. "Half a billion" may be as good a starting place as any for those of us who are trying to reconcile the creationist and scientist within, those of us who sense the holiness of creation while believing that raindrops could have fossilized in mud a billion years ago. The beauty of trying lies in the

10. Origen, *First Principles*, 189.

promise that this muddy, fossilized ground too is holy. And if we take our cues from those early church theologians and let Genesis open our eyes in another way, we know this ground, these origins—trilobites and all—are good, even "very good."

Time too. The truth is that the way Genesis counts in "days" and the way the scientific community counts in billions of years are both rather abstract. Einstein taught the world how intertwined time and space are in the universe, and I suspect there is a psychological version of the same truth. Time—all those sequences we can trace backward and forward in our minds—only becomes real to us in relation to the actual good stuff of creation: the lights in the sky, the limestone bluffs of the earth, and the primates that will eventually become human and discover trilobites and tell stories about the origins of the universe. And when time comes to life in such a way, it too is good.

I believe the Great River has been telling me so for years.

3

Life upon Life

STARING AT HALF A trilobite fossil, less than an inch long, and then scanning a hundred feet of limestone above—a weathered gray face of deep time and hidden stories—I began to think about all the shells and tiny bones of sea organisms and prehistoric vertebrates that it took to create such an immense wall, one six-thousand-year-old inch at a time. "A wall of life," I thought, realizing the bluff itself was once alive, and I could almost see it move. Perhaps it was the cool of a late autumn afternoon, but I shivered.

Strange things happen when considering life from within deep timeframes. In 14 billion years there is enough time to create 2 1/3 million universes that are six thousand years old. And like trilobites in limestone, there are sequences within sequences, stories within stories, universes within universes. And though "we cannot in one lifetime see all that we would like to see or learn all that we hunger to know," as Loren Eiseley suggests, "we have joined the caravan."[1] Ancient walls and shivers provide reminders, perhaps, that our roots rest so much deeper in creation than we can ever imagine. Deep time opens deep community.

Creations within Creation

Through the afternoon I teased out of my brother more timelines, and with them, a greater sense of the creations within creation. Between his accounts and my questions (with some later double-checking of dates) we were rehearsing an alternative version of the genesis of life on earth, one told in the texts of sediment and fossils.

1. Eiseley, *Immense Journey*, 12.

The trilobite we discovered was part of the *Cambrian explosion* occurring a half billion years ago, a period of relatively rapid growth in the
numbers and complexity of organisms appearing in the fossil record—all
once swarming around in ancient sea waters. And over the next 150 million
years, fish of all kinds began to fill the oceans with new forms of vertebrate
life. And even as the Great River is so threaded through our family's personal sense of origins, when considering how thoroughly the origins of all
life on earth are tied to water, I marvel. Water is home.

Even so, in this same period, between 500 and 350 million years ago,
another story was taking place, a great migration. Some adventurous plants
from these ancient oceans made an exodus, spreading onto the land, along
with some early insects. Over the next 100 million years, new types of am-
phibious creatures emerged, ones able to move in and out of the water and
utilize the oxygen found in the open air, paving the way for reptiles that
could make a home solely on land. Before long, from the perspective of
deep time, about 300 million years after those trilobites thrived, mammals,
birds, and all kinds of bugs came onto the scene, culminating with those
wild and fascinating dinosaurs who would reign over the planet for many
millions more.

Something wiped the dinosaurs out 65 million years ago, a comet perhaps, but it was not the first time that our world experienced such a great
loss in its populations. About 250 million years ago, in fact, something, or
some lethal combination of factors, wiped out most organic life, some 95
percent of all its forms by some estimates, including all descendents of the
trilobites. Nobody knows why for sure, but the best guesses point again
to comets or hyper-volcanic activity, that in turn heated the oceans and
released deadly amounts of methane. On the one hand, from the point of
view of evolution, life is incredibly persistent. On the other, we can also
see how incredibly fragile any one particular form of life can be, and how
thoroughly intertwined life is with its environmental home.

Of course I knew about the dinosaur extinction and even had a vague
sense of the timetables involved, but somehow the temporal implications
were only now catching up to me. Perhaps, again, it was the abstract character of pure numbers that emptied the impact, but now, with a sense of
these creatures lying about in the earth, even layering the earth, the numbers were coming to life. I began to imagine all the other reptiles, birds,
and mammals that managed to survive the trauma 65 million years ago, as
they commenced repopulating the earth, sparse at first like the animals of

Noah's ark, but soon filling the land and sky with new life. These land and sky creatures, along with marine life, have continued to evolve over these last 65 million years, getting us closer to the human chapter of the story.

The first primates seem to have evolved relatively soon after the extinction of the dinosaurs, maybe 50 to 60 million years ago. But think lemurs and shrews when imagining them, not monkeys. Monkeys will come a few million years later, with the first apes not appearing until about 25 million years ago. These apes in turn, over the last few million years, branch into a great variety of descendent species such as gorillas, chimps, bonobos, and humans.[2]

Enough. I decided not to ask any more questions of my brother. Not only were the numbers overwhelming, it was getting late and we were all getting hungry for Thanksgiving leftovers.

Dissociative Thinking

The truth is that even those of us who are part of religious communities that approach scriptures in more than literal ways are not, by and large, in the habit of searching among rocks and ancient riverbeds for the stories they could tell about the deep past. We are not accustomed to looking to the earth itself for insight into origins or the creative power at work through it all. In all my religious training and teaching, the words "consider the trilobite" have never entered a classroom. We like our texts, word-texts particularly. Rock-texts, and all that go with them, are new. Oddly, as beautiful and revelatory as our literatures and scriptures may be, this leaves us reflecting upon roughly the same time frame as our literalist cousins—the past few thousand years. No easy task in itself, but the more I have reflected upon this issue of time in relationship to human knowing, the more I see problems—even theological problems—our short time frames create.

When it comes to our own story as a species, when it comes to understanding the human mind as we know it—thinking, feeling, perceiving, consciousness, and more—we are jumping into the story at a very late stage. If we begin only a few thousand years ago, it is easy to assume that human beings have always had the same kind of mental life and conscious awareness that people have today. This is anything but a sure bet. Six thousand

2. For more detailed timelines and information, Smithsonian, "Geologic Time"; University of California Museum of Paleontology, "Online Exhibits"; and USGS, "Education," are helpful online resources.

years ago if we believe archeologists, paleontologists, and natural historians, too much has already occurred: people have spread all over the world, animals and crops have been domesticated, cities and temples built, music played, tools crafted, walls painted, figurines sculpted, the dead buried, and even calendars have been created. A lot of "mind stuff" has already occurred by the time anybody writes anything down.

So, when we open the book of knowing so late in the story, if we assume humans could always talk, write, build, farm, travel great distances, or pray, or if we simply forget there was a time when our ancestors could do none of these, it then becomes all too easy to exaggerate our differences with the rest of the creation, and miss the links. In other words, our relatively short time frames help eliminate the stories that associate us with other species and ultimately to our common origins. Perhaps this is one reason why those early church theologians—lacking larger time frames and the stories they contain—had to work so hard to defend the goodness of creation. Our know-it-all minds easily feed the narcissism of our species that wants to dissociate ourselves from the community of creation, wants to think of ourselves alone as special and good.

Though the Bible itself warns of the dangers of such self-importance, unfortunately much in the history of Western thought has contributed to an overly heightened view of ourselves. Humans are the special, spiritual creatures, set apart with souls, who alone reflect the image of God; the rest of reality is composed of nothing more than individual atoms, lacking the life-giving breath of God. Even theories of knowledge have reflected such dissociative assumptions, even down to the level of the senses. The world we sense through our bodies, as Plato believed, is nothing but a flat deception, like two-dimensional shadows on a cave wall. Consequently, to know truth, our minds need to dissociate from our bodies and fill in the gaps and depths to find the truth.[3] Our hx-ical bias. Western ...

At its worst, thinking and knowing bolstered by such a view of reality serve to break down the world we encounter, to divide and conquer the world to be known, not only to understand it, but to control and manipulate it as well. The mind becomes "a mercenary of our will to power," as

---

3. It was not until the 1960s and 70s, primarily through the work of experimental psychologists J. J. and Eleanor Gibson and their "ecological approach" to perception, that these assumptions about how the senses work were themselves finally revealed to be flat, reflecting some bad assumptions, if not human hubris. See James Gibson, *Ecological Approach*; and Eleanor Gibson, *Perceptual Learning*. See also Wigger, *Texture*, for a description and analysis of this work.

Abraham Heschel puts it, "trained to assail in order to plunder rather than to commune in order to love."[4] Here, to know is to dominate, to possess, to absorb, to colonize. Knowledge is power, reducing reality to, in Loren Eiseley's words, "the chill void of ever-streaming particles."[5]

The implication is that human knowing cut off from its deep past is too easily tempted by the devil of dissociation. Dissociated from creation, we see the world as if through a pinhole and we find ourselves wandering outside the gates of Eden. The minister in me worries that our dissociative ways cut us off from the sacred origin of life. The moralist in me worries that in an age of such massive power, dissociation breeds and feeds mass destruction.

Knowing in Relationship

To recognize ourselves as part of a community of creation, as Jürgen Molt-mann describes it, is more than sentimental wording, more than a romantic notion of nature. The phrase instead is used very intentionally by the theologian to do fuller justice to the nature of life itself and our ways of knowing the world of which we are part. Over the past century, particularly, with the development of the physical and biological sciences, a dissociative, isolationist, atomistic picture of the universe has been collapsing. Instead, "Objects can be known and understood very much better if they are seen in their relationships and co-ordinations with their particular environments and surroundings (which include the human observer)—if, that is to say, they are integrated, not isolated; perceived in their totality, not split up."[6]

From the relationship between space and time to the strange world of quantum physics, even the hardest of sciences paints a highly relational picture of the universe. And the difference between understanding reality through relationships, or not, is the difference between life and death. "To be alive means existing in relationship with other people and things." And conversely, "isolation and lack of relationship means death for all living things, and dissolution even for elementary particles." To know anything, then, is to understand life "in its relationships, interconnections and surroundings."[7] This includes knowing ourselves and our abilities to know.

4. Heschel, *Man Is Not Alone*, 38.

5. Loren Eiseley, *Star Thrower*, 190.

6. Moltmann, *God in Creation*, 2–3.

7. Ibid., 3.

The religious imagination has much to gain from science on this front. Perspectives born of studying natural history and evolution, for example, potentially put the human knower into a larger environment of time and space alike, helping us all better see ourselves in relationship to the world, not separate from, but deeply embedded in the community of creation.

When religious texts and ideas are allowed to breathe a little, where belief allows the grandeur of creation to humble humanity, there grows the possibility that the larger time frames a scientific imagination offers can bear good fruit. In short, to see in time its deeper possibilities is to begin to recognize the relationships. To hear the stories, and the stories within stories that the heavens and earth tell, is to honor the kinship. To explore whatever may be original to human knowing in relation to our common origins with all of creation is to celebrate the community. "Everything exists, lives and moves in others, in one another, for one another, in the cosmic interrelations of the divine Spirit."[8] From this theological point of view, *creation* is more than a doctrine or creed or even more than a theory of origins. Instead creation is an expression of faith—a way of knowing even—flowing from a profound sense of communion with the known. "In perceiving the world as creation," says Moltmann, "the human being discerns and enters into a community of creation."[9]

Paradoxically, staring into the darkness of a deep past may actually allow us to see through the glass of knowing a little more clearly, past our own reflection, in order to recognize ourselves as part of a great community of life, "a creature in the history of creation."[10] As scientists of various sorts dig into our deep past on earth, little by little, creature by creature, bone by bone, seed by seed, speck of pollen by speck of pollen, a wonderfully strange thing happens. Time opens and with it deep community.

Telling the stories in a few paragraphs, pages, and chapters may not be much of an improvement over not telling it at all, but it's a beginning, and if we let it, one that reminds us our roots rest much deeper in creation than many of us have ever imagined.

8. Ibid., 11.
9. Ibid., 70.
10. Ibid., 185.

Part I: Origins

∞

As the light from the sun, that five-billion-year-old friend of the earth, began yielding its rule on this day after Thanksgiving, the temporal shock of considering creatures half a billion years old softened slightly, though did not go away completely. Looking around, it was enough for the moment to feel connected to it all—creations living and dead in whose midst I was standing. Connected to the river, those waters of life; connected to the bluffs, composed of millions of years of life; connected to my family, through whom life continues.

Time to go home.

PART II

ROOTS, ROCKS, AND RELATIONSHIPS

"And this is our root," declares the Ancient Word. Through hieroglyphics etched into stone centuries ago, if not millennia, the Quiché Maya of the Guatemalan highlands tell how the gods created the first humans on earth.[1] It took four tries.

The first attempt failed because the creatures could not speak, and therefore could not name or praise their makers; they just squawked and chattered, howled and moaned, and this disappointed the gods. So these became "the animals on the face of the earth."

The gods tried again, this time with mud, to make a creature that would praise and respect them, people who could provide for and nurture one another; but this mud-creature's body kept crumbling and dissolving and it could not talk sense. So they let it dwindle away.

Next the gods sculpted humankind from wood, and these folk could indeed speak and multiply and fill the earth, however, there was nothing in their hearts or in their minds; there was no memory of their makers. So Hurricane crushed them with a giant rainstorm and their descendents become the monkeys.[2]

The gods tried yet again, using ground corn. Finally it worked. Four men and four women are eventually created—the first mother-fathers— good and beautiful people who can walk and talk, multiply and fill the earth, and most of all can give thanks to their Builders, their Masons. "Double thanks, triple thanks," say the first corn people to the Maker, Modeler:

1. The story is told in the *Popol Vuh*, literally "The Council Book," a work translated by an anonymous group of Quiché lords in the 16th century, based upon earlier hieroglyphic versions now lost to history. The quotes here are from Dennis Tedlock's English translation.

2. Tedlock, *Popol Vuh*, 78–86.

"Thanks to you we've been formed, we've come to be made and modeled, our grandmother, our grandfather."[3]

The gods had succeeded, had perfected their craft. But as it turns out, the new creatures were too perfect. The people were able to see and know all, understanding everything perfectly, and this threatened the superiority of the gods. So the gods fogged up their vision and weakened their human eyes so that they could only see things that are nearby. Their means of perfect knowledge was thereby lost.[4]

If it were not for the Ancient Word, the *Popol Vuh*, a book based upon those ancient hieroglyphs, we still would not be able to see beyond the present into this foggy past.

∞

"And this is our root," offers the Popol Vuh, "we who are the Quiché people."[5]

3. Ibid., 166.
4. Ibid., 166–67.
5. Ibid., 167.

4

Etchings

Karen Armstrong's
a History of God

ENCOUNTERS WITH TRILOBITES AND rivers, with limestone and ancient texts, have not only rocked my sense of time out of a nearsighted present, but continue to stir my curiosity over our origins, our root, our dawning as a species somewhere in a past that we can only see from afar and never with pure clarity. Who are our ancient ancestors and where and when did they live? How long ago was it? And what did they know or think about? Was there anything in their hearts or minds? Were they able, once upon a time, to see all? Did they at some point bite from a know-it-all tree? Or did they swing from it?

A larger sense of time invites more and more questions, and I have found myself scouring the current etchings of anthropologists and paleontologists for a contemporary Word to supplement the ancient, all in order to better understand where we come from and how we have come to a place in time in which we can ask big questions about our own origins and try to answer them with words old and new. The drive to understand our genesis, the need to identify those earliest ancestors, is nearly universal and is perhaps a key feature of human knowing itself.[1] It is as if that sense of *I* or *me* needs to know the *we* or *us* of our origins whether they are our parents, Adam and Eve, or the Quiché mother-fathers.

Unlike the sea turtle that, once hatching, races to the ocean never knowing its egg-laying mother, the human child reaches out immediately for connection to its source, at first for a visceral immediate kind of

---

1. A fascinating exception seems to be the Pirahã of Brazil, who do not appear to have origin stories and do not trace their ancestors any farther back than living memory. See Everett, "Cultural Constraints." Everett makes the case that this is a cultural phenomenon raising suspicion about "universal grammar."

knowledge through the body itself. Later the child reaches for more complex and indirect kinds of knowledge through ideas, memories, and all kinds of symbol making, such as stories that tell us where we come from, and from whom, and from whom they come, and so on until we reach some sort of origin of origins.

The fact that people argue so much about these stories—about how long ago we can reach back or whether apes or Adam and Eve or the gods were involved—only testifies to how much a sense of who we are is tied to our beliefs about who we were. We are made to seek our origins. Yet vision is foggy. Interpreting rocks and fossils or primitive stone tools and cave paintings from the past is every bit as tricky as interpreting Scripture, a work of art, or even a bodily gesture is today. Still, the drive to know remains.

our brain's desire to shortcut/ settle on certainty

An Evolving Story

Even as creationists have been trying to prove the truth of a young universe, the world of science continues to dig up bones, date carbon isotopes, and study the stars in a way that has been expanding our knowledge of the universe and rewriting the story of human origins. But because the characters are so old, so well hidden in the earth, and so complex, the tale has been, and continues to be, a work in progress.

For example, even as William Jennings Bryan was about to square off with Clarence Darrow over John Scopes teaching evolution in 1925 Dayton, Tennessee, anthropologists and paleontologists were just as fiercely fighting with themselves over the claims of an article published in the journal *Nature*. The debate involved a section of limestone, this one thousands of miles away from the bluffs of Southern Illinois, a chunk mined from a quarry in South Africa. Professor Raymond Dart was claiming he had discovered hard evidence of a creature that seemed to be part human and part ape.[2]

Theories of our connection to other primates had been around for some time, but evidence was sketchy at best. Even before Charles Darwin published his first book on evolution, *On the Origin of the Species*, in 1859,[3] bones from what appeared to be an earlier type of human had

2. Dart, "*Australopithicus.*"

3. Darwin did not address human evolution specifically until the later work *The Descent of Man* (1871).

been discovered in the Neander Valley of Germany. Now thought to be approximately 40 thousand years old, there was, however, no agreement about what the Neanderthal was or how it related to humans, let alone to apes. The discovery of a thirty-thousand-year-old so-called Cro-Magnon skull in France in 1868 didn't help, as it looked even more human. Though fascinating discoveries, without stronger evidence the human-ape connection was more speculation than established fact.

All that changed in 1924. As professor Dart chipped away at a block of rock from the quarry at the town of Taungs, he began to realize what lay before him. He spent over two months freeing the fossil of what should have been, given its size, an ape skull. But, two things were wrong. First of all, the teeth—they were distinctly human. Secondly, the opening at the base of the skull, the opening for the spinal cord, revealed that this creature walked upright—unlike any other ape.

Later nicknamed the Taung Child, Dart announced that he had discovered a new species that fell into the gap between an older species of apes and human beings. He named it *Australopithecus africanus*, that is, the "southern ape of Africa." Though the Taung Child lived only a short time, dying at only three or four years of age, the issue of when the child lived was the startling news—over two million years ago. And therein lay the debate. Even Dart's own mentors did not believe it and the claim was, by and large, rejected. The dating at 2.3 million years in the past was simply too long ago.

Dart's discovery not only contradicted a creationist worldview but also any notion that—likely influenced by colonialist assumptions—humanity came out of Europe, not out of Africa. But with the help of several more discoveries over the next two decades to follow, including an adult version of the same species, the professor and the Taung Child were finally vindicated and *Australopithecus* was accepted as a genuine link between modern humans and our ape ancestors, a link that expanded our history way beyond a time frame of thousands of years to that of millions of years.

If Darwin's theory of evolution represents a first step in humanity waking up to itself in relation to its primate past, this little child from South Africa represents step two.

Since Dart's discovery, more and more paleontologists and anthropologists have been hunting and digging in Africa in search of more clues to our ancestry. The efforts are working too. The picture of our origins gets more and more intriguing each decade, if not each year, as new discoveries are made. The story itself is a bit messy, full of riddles, and is still itself evolving.

Beyond the expanding time frame, one of the difficulties understanding our origins has to do with the sheer variety of relevant fossils that have been found. While they are collectively known as hominids (sharing some combination of human and ape appearance), many of them are different enough from each other in such features as brain size or jaw structure, that they are considered separate species within the general category of hominids.[4]

Contrary to the iconic depiction of evolution involving one species transforming into another into another in a straight line from monkey to modern human, several of these hominid varieties existed simultaneously. For example, while the Taung Child's species (*Australipithicus africanus*) was walking the earth 2.5 million years ago, so was the smaller-brained *Australipithicus aethipicus* (first discovered in Ethiopia in the 1960s). At times there were as many as a half dozen or more different hominid species populating Africa at the same time, primates who fall somewhere between ape and human. And as more and more fossils are discovered, we could possibly learn there were even more species, along with more overlap between them.

In other words, if you were to create an image of evolution these days, it would look more like a flowchart or a genealogical tree branching out in multiple directions. The Taung Child revealed that the trunk was over two million years old. Yet, it turns out that the trunk is even older still. After 1974, hominid history began reaching even farther back.

Lucy

In 1974, Donald Johanson led a dig in the Afar region of Ethiopia and there discovered the fossilized bones of a hominid unique enough to warrant a new name, *Austalopithecus afarensis*, that is, "southern ape of Afar."[5] That night there was a celebration party in camp complete with a tape recording of the Beatles song "Lucy in the Sky with Diamonds" playing over and over

---

4. Here "hominid" will refer to the various species of great apes descending from the last ancestor shared with, but not including, chimps and bonobos. For a discussion of the terminology debates, see Berger, "Viewpoint."

5. See Johanson and Taieb, "Plio-Pleistocene Hominid."

again. The bones took on the nickname Lucy.[6] Far from the sky in fact, Lucy had been resting in the earth for 3.2 million years. And before she rested in it, according to Johanson, she walked upright upon the earth, that is, nearly a million years before the Taung Child.

Walking upright is a compelling focus to students of evolution not only because other apes do not do it, not regularly; walking upright is believed to signal less dependence upon heavy forests for a primary habitat. The species could travel longer distances for food and water, if necessary, and perhaps even take advantage of food sources in woodlands and grassy savannahs. It is the evolutionary equivalent of the difference between crawling and walking in a baby. As any parent can testify, the range of mobility (and potential trouble) increases exponentially the steadier the child becomes on his feet.

To some, Johanson's claim regarding Lucy's gait was sketchy, based as it was on her knee joint. In addition, like the Taung Child, Lucy had a relatively small brain, like a chimp, and some felt that upright walking would require a larger brain. But only a few years later, in 1978, Mary Leakey provided even more compelling evidence with her discovery of actual footprints among Lucy's kind. While of the same species, the footprints Leakey found in the hardened volcanic ash of Laetoli, Tanzania, turned out to be even older than Lucy herself at an estimated 3.5 to 3.7 million years old. It was sure proof that *Australopithecus afarensis* walked upright, and in Leakey's words, the footprints are clear evidence that "bipedalism outstripped enlargement of the brain."[7] We walked first and got a bigger brain later.

In Leakey's original 1979 article describing the Laetoli footprints, she reveals another reason why walking upright is significant to piecing together the story of human evolution. Walking upright is a major event in evolution because it "freed the hands for tool-making and eventually led to more sophisticated human activities."[8]

6. To hear Johanson describe the discovery in his own words, go to Johanson, *Becoming Human*.

7. Leakey and Hay, "Pliocene Footprints," 323.

8. Ibid.

Bodies and Knowledge

Now this is the point where the story of human origins becomes particularly relevant for students of human knowing. If indeed our story involves a gradual transformation from creatures who climb more than walk to creatures who can make tools, imagine the future, or build space vehicles, the assumption is that something changes mentally as well as physically to allow all of this to happen. Human cognition, human thinking, the mind, and intelligence are all ways of talking about the realm or capacity that works out these "more sophisticated human activities."

In other words, the mind has a history. Thinking has a root. If one is open to an evolutionary framework for understanding our past, then not only have our bodies evolved, our minds have too. And in this evolution of the cognitive life through time may be clues to understanding ourselves better as knowing bodies today.

So, given the importance of this hands-free moment in our story, what was it that Leakey found in the fossilized volcanic ash to support the idea that walking upright was the birth of tool-making? Did she find an axe? A projectile point? A club? No. Actually there was nothing but the footprints, no signs of any handmade artifacts whatsoever.

Leakey provides two possible explanations. One is that these hominids made tools, but that they made them from sticks or other materials that have long since perished. The other possibility is that "the concept of tool-making may well have been beyond the mental ability of these small-brained creatures."[9] So while a larger brain may not have been essential for walking upright, it may have been essential for these other forms of behavior that we eventually call human—from tool-making, cave painting, and writing to debating the origins of life, explaining the northern lights, or praising the Quiché Builders.

Since the 1970s many more hominid fossils have been found in Africa, and with them new varieties of *Australopithecus*.[10] To date, the oldest is the four-million-year-old *Australopithecus anamensis*, identified in 1995 by another generation of Leakeys digging in Kenya, and it appears that all more recent hominids, including the line that leads directly to modern humans, go through this four-million-year-old.[11]

9. Ibid.
10. For example, *A. robustus, A. gahri*, and *A. boisei*.
11. See M. G. Leakey, et al., "New Specimens."

But other species of hominids have also been discovered, species that are so different that they are not considered to be part of the *Australopithecus* genus. They are hominids because they too share both human and ape features. Some are more recent descendants, such as the two-million-year-old *Paranthropus boisei* and *Paranthropos robustus*, and some are older, such as the 4.4-million-year-old *Ardipithecus ramidus* (nicknamed Ardi) discovered in Ethiopia.[12] But at this point the lines get very blurry and the fossil record is as debated among paleontologists as the Bible is among its scholars and theologians. The lines get blurry in part because there may have been several variations of hominids/apes in this period, not just one clean line.[13] And the fossils are still too few and far between to make confident, let alone absolute, determinations.

What is becoming clearer and clearer though, from these fossil finds, is that several species of hominids were not only in the southern regions of the continent, but all over Africa, and for millions of years.

As I write, the candidate for the oldest possible hominid ancestor, though murky, involves a fossil discovery in the early 21st century by Michel Brunet and colleagues in the Sahel region of Chad. Nicknamed Toumai, which means "the hope of life" in the local Goran language, *Sahelanthropus tchadensis* lived somewhere between six and seven million years ago. The murkiness has to do with the fact that the back of the skull looks like a chimp's while the front looks like a much more recent (1.75-million-year-old) australopithecine.[14]

Where and when to draw the lines between hominids and early chimpanzees will likely be debated in the decades, if not centuries, to come, with each unearthed fossil. There simply is not enough information currently to resolve these issues. Of course this leaves gaps in the story. But for those of us who spend more time with ancient word-texts than with ancient bones, this is nothing new. Interpretation continues and expands with each new discovery, whether it is a detail that has always been overlooked or a major find, from punctuation marks to the Dead Sea Scrolls. In the case of human origins, the gaps—to my mind—only increase the expectation that each fossil dig could help us understand ourselves, our roots, a little bit better.

---

12. White, et al., "*Australopithecus ramidus*."

13. In addition some paleontologists are debating whether *ramidus* (Ardi) is even a hominid or some other type of similar ape that is now extinct and without descendents.

14. See Wood, "Paleoanthropology."

In all, the general scientific consensus now is that somewhere in Africa about 25 million years ago a species of great apes broke off from the larger monkey family. About 12 million years ago we still shared a common ancestor with orangutans, and 8 to 10 million years ago, with gorillas. Now it looks as if somewhere between six and seven million years ago there was an ape that was the ancestor of all hominids, all those mentioned above, including the line of hominids that eventually becomes us. This ancestor is common to all humans and is also the ancestor of all chimps and bonobos today. Those great apes went one way on all fours. We walked another on two.

Whether or not this six-to-seven-million-year-old primate Eve was made of mud, wood, or corn flour is a matter for debate.

5

The Hatchet

IF THE HOMINID STORY begins somewhere between six and seven million years ago, Lucy brings us halfway home to the present, the Taung Child slightly closer. So what has happened since? What has happened with the family of hominids from the time of the australopithecines until the time when the only remaining descendents of hominids are of the species known as *Homo sapiens*, that is, the "knowing" or "wise" human? This period, the last 2 to 2.5 million years, is one in which some of the most dramatic changes in hominid history have occurred, and the changes occur not only in the bodies of hominids, but presumably in their minds as well, in their ability to think, to communicate, to make things, and to reflect upon their world.

Tools

Imagine for a moment a hatchet. The one I have in mind was my grandfather's and I use it a handful of times a year to chop kindling in the winter. It's steel, with a handle wrapped in rubber that is all cracked and dried from 50 years, maybe more, of use. It has a leather sheath, torn and coming apart at the seams, and it won't last much longer. The hatchet, for me, is a sweet reminder of my grandfather and even the shed where he kept it—I can almost smell it—as well as the camping trips we made when I was very young, as he used the hatchet to build fires in which to cook wonderful dessert pies my grandmother prepared in these cast iron molds we could put right into the flame.

Imagine that you have such a hatchet, and maybe you do, but now consider that this is the only tool in your entire life. I don't mean "tool" as imers and saws and screwdrivers. I mean "tool" in the larger sense human implement, any human-made object of any sort, from refrig-... rs and televisions to cars, telephones, toys, books, lights, windows, or pillows. You have neither nifty cast iron molds for baking pies, nor even a campfire. Look around your home and notice all that would not be there, including the chair you read in. Walk down your street and notice what would not be there—the more urban your dwelling, the more dramatic the difference would be. Envision the sort of life you would have walking around with only your hatchet, and picture how different it would be from your current life. And now suppose that the hatchet isn't even very sharp, in fact, it's not made of steel, but stone—looking more like a broken rock with some jagged edges for chopping, just big enough to hold in your hand.

Welcome to the world of *Homo habilis*, the so-called "handy" or "able" human, who lived between 2.5 and 1.5 million years ago, the species discovered by Dr. Louis Leakey in the early 1960s, and for what it's worth, the first hominid to receive the human (*Homo*) designation rather than ape (*pithecus*).[1]

To put matters in perspective, for somewhere around four million years, hominids survived just fine without any type of hatchet, any rock choppers, or other such implements. It is certainly possible that our ancestors—as chimps sometimes do today—would use leaves to collect water to drink, or would swing a stick at a tree limb to knock down some fruit, but we have no way of knowing whether they did or not. Or perhaps, unlike other apes, earlier hominids scraped sticks into simple spears or knives, but we cannot know this either since such wooden tools would have perished long ago.

So all we know for sure is that these stone choppers—called cores— as well as the chips coming off the cores—called flakes—start showing up some 2.5 million years ago with the remains of *Homo habilis*. Why the change? And what could it say about the mind who invented the tools in the first place?

Worlds of Change

Ordinarily there is little incentive for a species to initiate any great change in its patterns of behavior. In fact change can be dangerous, throwing the ecological niche of the species far out of kilter. A new, more efficient way

1. L.S.B Leakey, et al., "New Species," 8. why our b = Δ w/anx?

of gathering fruits and nuts, for example, could lead to a thriving hominid population in an area, at least for a while. But too many hominids pressuring an area could lead to fewer birds or bugs or bees that pollinate the trees and plants that provided the food in the first place. Easy for contemporary humans—*Homo technologicus*—to miss this, we who can manipulate the environment so easily, have done so for so long, and who address unintended consequences of technological innovation with more innovation. So while there could be many reasons our ancestors began making and using these simple stone choppers, a good bet is that the development arose in response to changes already occurring in the environment. And in fact the appearance of stone tools does seem to coincide with changes in the earth's climate, and with it, the vegetation and fauna of our planet.[2]

Somewhere between two and three million years ago the planet experienced the beginning of one of its major ice ages. As icy glaciers began to crawl farther and farther south into places like Europe and North America, Africa too cooled off. But our hominid forbearers were never threatened with the kind of tundra conditions created in the north; they would never have seen a glacier.[3] Even so, there was a problem, a problem that could easily have forced a major change in behavior and eventually in the family tree. The problem was less rain. Forests began to shrink dramatically and so did the supply of fruits and nuts and tubers that Lucy would have relied upon for food. Over the next few hundred millennia to come, the strict vegetarian diet of hominids would have been tough to survive on, especially as competition for the dwindling resources increased. Some of our ancestors would have had to find new sources of food energy to supplement or replace the nuts and fruits that had worked so well for millions of years previously. And it appears that some did.

While the forests shrank, the grasslands grew, and so did certain animal populations that could thrive on grass, such as zebras and antelopes. Grass grazers could flourish. But, so could those meat-eating creatures that could hunt among theses herds or scavenge their remains—lions and jackals, for example, and as it turns out, some of Lucy's descendants. Roughly 2.5 million years ago, it appears that our ancestors were eating the meat and perhaps the bone marrow of these grass-eating animals, thereby providing themselves with a rich source of calories. One reason we know that they

---

2. On the relationship between climate change and hominid changes, I am following Calvin, *Brief History*, especially ch. 3.

3. Ibid., 23–24.

were—cut marks on the bones of the prey. Someone was using the broken edges of stones to scrape the meat from the bones of animals.[4]

So far the earliest types of tools that have been discovered are those cores and flakes found along with the bones of *Homo habilis*. The implements are classified as Olduwan tools, named for the area where they and *habilis* were first discovered, the Oduvai Gorge of Tanzania. Paleontologists debate whether the original rock core or the flakes were more important. The core could be used to chop open bones or scrape meat for example; the flakes that are chipped off would also be sharp enough to cut through skin and muscle.[5] Either way, the appearance of these cores and flakes, along with piles of animal bones bearing their use, marks the beginning of a Stone Age and a clear indication that our ancestors had begun to make tools.

The theory is that this ice age led to the Stone Age, with the Stone Age reflecting a major transition in the behavior and presumably the mind of one branch of the hominid tree, a branch that eventually leads on to modern humans.

Bigger Brains

Based upon the skull size, we know the brain of *habilis* was much larger than anything that had come before. On the surface, this larger brain seems

4. See ibid., chs. 3–4.

5. See Klein and Edgar, *Dawn*, ch. 3.

to be a reasonable explanation for why tool-making begins to show up. A new, more cognitively creative, bigger-brained species comes along and invents this ingenious method for getting at the meat and marrow of a carcass more efficiently, and I might add, more quickly, in light of any lions lingering around. A bigger brain leads to bigger ideas. Logical enough.

But maybe not. There's a twist. Since that original discovery among *Homo habilis*, Olduwan tools have been discovered even earlier—2.6 million years ago—with the smaller-brained *Australopithecus*. It looks as if the tools actually come before the bigger brains (and this is confusing because the tools come before the species that was actually named for using them). As William Calvin explains in his book *A Brief History of the Mind*: "First it's toolmaking, then the spinoff." As he puts it, "Behavior invents, using the klutzy old anatomy, then anatomy slowly changes to make the new behavior more efficient via the usual Darwinian process."[6] In other words the practice of tool-making may have led or contributed to the development of a species who was better at the practice, those with the physical dexterity to be skilled at the task and the mental dexterity to learn and remember how to do it. Maybe a bigger brain helped, aided by the rich new source of calories, but the bigger brain followed rather than led the way.

Strange to think that human beings could be here today because some hominid—between the time of Lucy and the Taung Child—began using rocks to break and scrape bones. And, significantly, we are here because the practice stuck long enough to change the bodies of our ancestors.

∞

To summarize our hominid family story, for the first four million years or so—well over half of our hominid time on earth—there are no stone tools, we were vegetarian, and our brains were much smaller. Between two and three million years ago, as the planet was cooling and African forests were shrinking, simple stone choppers and their flakes start showing up, along with cut marks on animal bones, as well as a new species of hominids. Calvin calls this period one of "triple startups"—tools, ice, and bigger brains.[7] And this triple startup is a good reminder of something difficult to notice, as the *Popol Vuh* would put it, from the nearsighted view of the present. That is, from the farsighted view of deep time, measured in hundreds of

6. Calvin, *Brief History*, 27.
7. Ibid., 23.

thousands of years, it is much easier to see how thoroughly intertwined are creation, body, and mind.

Aping Behavior

In the world of anthropology, tool-making is generally understood to represent the first sure sign of human culture. That is, the practice of making tools reveals that something besides genes could be passed along from one generation to the next without dying out—a kind of knowledge, a set of behaviors that endures beyond the first generation. For example: how to make the tools, how to use them, what kind of rocks work best, where to find them. Richard Dawkins has dubbed such cultural knowledge *memes*, to echo the word *genes*, and the practice of making tools would be a good, if not the earliest known, example. While it may well be that such passing along of knowledge and behavior happened long before this time—it probably did—but like wooden tools we have no evidence. Lucy, for example, may have learned from her parents to watch the sunset every evening and then do three back flips while screeching, but we have no way of knowing this now. Behaviors without artifacts leave no signs, which is to say that with some matters we will be forever nearsighted.

now = videos gone viral

Steven Mithen, in his *Prehistory of the Mind*, sees stone tool-making as the first sign of what he calls a "technical intelligence" among all the great ape descendents. The kind of controlled force and appreciation of angles necessary to create early tools represents a type of "intuitive physics," as he calls it, not seen anywhere else in the ape world. Making these choppers would not only require a finer-grained hand dexterity, he reasons, it represents a genuine cognitive, mental breakthrough in the species.[8]

Mithen may be right; even domesticated apes that are shown how are not good at learning to make stone tools.[9] But not everyone agrees that tool-making is the great mental breakthrough or sign of originality. Tool-making, more modestly, could simply be a version of the ways in which all kinds of creatures modify their environments. Termites build mounds, moles tunnel, birds piece together nests, and beavers construct huts and dams. Closer to evolutionary home, chimps, in addition to using leaves to collect water or sticks to knock down fruit, have also been seen stripping the leaves off small branches in order to "fish" for termites. That is, they

8. Mithen, *Prehistory*, 96–98.
9. Ibid.; Klein and Edgar, *Dawn*, 73–74.

stick the barren twig down the termite hill and then pull it back up to collect the bugs to eat. So the question is whether or not crafting a stone tool and termite fishing are of the same cognitive fabric. Not an easy question to answer.

If tool-making is simply a matter of modifying the environment or objects in the environment for food or habitat, then stone tools may not be so special. But what if the significance of the emerging practice in the species has more to do with how such behavior becomes established and how long it lasts? What if uniqueness has more to do with the way tool-making is passed along from one generation to the next? Some of the most fascinating work on this front has been done by Michael Tomasello and his associates who have done extensive studies and experiments in the area of human cognition as well as the cognition of other primates generally, including our closest relatives, chimpanzees. Having written books on both primate cognition and human cognition, Tomasello is in one of the best positions of any scholar to evaluate what is original and what is not in human knowing.[10] So what does he see?

When Tomasello considers termite fishing and other examples of tool use among chimps, he indeed sees these as intelligent behaviors that reflect cognitive skills that may have been and may continue to be very helpful for survival. At the same time, he also concludes that tool-making among other species of primates is of a different type of intelligence than that which happens cognitively when humans (and perhaps earlier hominids) make tools. They are, we might say, different kinds of smart. The key difference is imitation. Chimps are not so great at it. *mirror neurons*

Despite the common conception that "aping" behavior is imitative behavior, it looks as if humans, at least those of the current species, are the best imitators. Chimps seem to be paying attention less to the behavior of others, and more to what Tomasello calls the *dynamic affordances* of the environment. What does that mean?

As an example of a dynamic affordance, Tomasello describes the situation in which a child chimp sees her mother roll a log and eat the insects she finds underneath. The child may well start rolling logs to find insects herself, but it is only because she learned that there are insects under the log. That is, the environment affords something to eat under logs. The key for Tomasello is that the child already could roll logs, could already eat bugs,

10. Good summary examples of this work are Tomasello's *Cultural Origins* and *Primate Cognition*.

Part II: Roots, Rocks, and Relationships

and did not need the mother in order to learn to do these things. As he says, "the youngster would have learned the same thing if the wind, rather than her mother, had caused the log to roll over and expose the ants."[11] The *apes* emphasis is on opportunities the environment and environmental events afford, not upon the behavior of the other. *opportunistic*

The difference is subtle to be sure, but an experiment conducted by Katherine Nagel, Raquel Olguin, and Tomasello himself helps to illustrate the stakes at work in such a subtlety.[12] This research team devised a situation to study and compare chimps with two-year-old human children. The heart of the experiment involved the chimps and children trying to obtain out-of-reach objects through an opening in some fencing.

These kinds of experiments have been going on for nearly a century, ever since the Wolfgang Kohler began hanging food out of the reach of chimps to see whether they could figure out a way to get at it. And they would, stacking boxes or using sticks to do so. At the time it seemed to reveal that animals were much more capable of "intelligence" and "insight" than many thought, especially in the wake of experiments like Pavlov's dogs and Skinner's pigeons, which seemed to show nothing but automated behavior.

Nagel's team put a clever twist on these old insight experiments, however. They would actually demonstrate to the chimps and toddlers how to use a small rake to obtain the objects (food in the case of chimps, and a small toy in the case of children). But the even bigger twist was that they demonstrated using the tool in two different ways to different groups to see what would happen.

The teeth of this rake were relatively long and far apart, so if you tried to gather the food or toy with the teeth down, like raking leaves, the food would easily and often slip through the tines. It could eventually do the job, but very inefficiently. The rake worked perfectly well, however, if turned upside down—teeth up—because the solid base could bring the desired object right to the chimp or child. So to some children and some chimps, the researcher demonstrated the inefficient method. And to other chimps and children the researchers demonstrated the efficient method. The results: whether shown the efficient or inefficient way, the chimps would employ the efficient method; that is, chimps would keep or turn the teeth of the

---

11. Tomasello *Cultural Origins*, 29.

12. Nagell et al., "Processes of Social Learning."

rake up to bring the food on in. Two-year-old humans, on the other hand, did whatever the demonstrator did, whether efficient or not.

Nagel and company conclude that the chimps and children were paying attention to two different aspects of the situation, each complex in its own way. The chimps were most attentive to the "general functional relations in the task and to the results," in other words, how to get the job done. The two-year-olds, on the other hand, "were focused on the demonstrator's actual method of tool use (her behavior)."[13]

From Generation to Generation

As Tomasello points out, this human style of imitative learning and the cognition at work in it should not be considered a "higher" or "more intelligent" strategy than what the chimps do. In fact, you could make the opposite argument if speed and efficiency are key (which are in fact rewarded on most scholastic and intelligence tests). Instead, the human style of imitative learning is a more social strategy, "which, in some circumstances and for some behaviors, has some advantages."[14] I would consider it, following the work of Howard Gardner's theory of multiple intelligences, as reflecting a kind of social or interpersonal intelligence, a particular attunement to the behaviors of others in a way that lets us follow suit.[15] Chimps may be more insightful than toddlers when figuring out the possibilities an environment affords, while the toddlers may be more so when it comes to behavior. Each kind of intelligence or insight or strategy has its place in the world of primates; each has served the survival of a species in various environmental niches.

Making tools and then sustaining tool-making practices over time seems to be one of those circumstances for which this more social strategy of humans has advantages. Chimp tool use, if that is even the right term, is sporadic, tends to die out easily, and depends much more upon trial and error, as well as the particular idiosyncrasies of the terrain.[16] In a sense, chimps continually reinvent based upon what an environment affords. Humans, by imitating, participate in a kind of recursive, social loop for the species, and therefore do not have to continually reinvent.

13. Ibid., 174.
14. Tomasello, *Cultural Origins*, 30.
15. See Gardner, *Frames*, especially ch. 10.
16. Tomasello, *Cultural Origins*, ch. 2.

Possibly the most persuasive piece of evidence along these lines is another feature of the tool-making fossil record. Those simple Olduwan cores and flakes do not only show up in the fossil record for a generation or two, some 2.6 million years ago. These tools continue to be made for a million years, and remarkably, with very little variation across space or time. And precisely because the same style of tool lasts for so long with so little variation—something I still have trouble comprehending—suggests that imitation was indeed more important than innovation.

While some sort of creativity would have been key to the origins of a new behavior such as using a sharp stone to scrape meat off a bone, imitation appears to be the key that allows the initially creative behavior to endure past the first generation.[17] So, as much as our current technological culture prizes creativity, innovation, and originality, a large component of learning and education still rests in our proficiency at imitation, whether we are learning language, how to dance, hit a baseball, paint, act, sing, how to treat others, or pray. Whether from schoolteachers, parents, or others we look to, the seeds of education are rooted deeply in our powers of imitation, which in turn are rooted in a deep, socially sensitive past.

another leap-cognitive brain dev.

v.v. important

17. Ibid., 39.

6

Promethean Moments

"YOU KNOW THERE'S A theory," my friend Chip was offering as I splintered a piece of silver maple with my grandfather's hatchet, "that beer is the root of civilization." Over a small fire our conversation had wandered from the Grateful Dead and the Beatles to Lucy and the Stone Age and the origins of everything until we finally landed on one of our one of our favorite subjects.

Putting down the hatchet, I added the fresh fuel to the fire, sat on an upturned log, and took a generous drink of our latest batch of homebrew. "Yep, I believe," I answered even though neither of us really did, "especially if it tasted like this." The beer was good and I knew the theory: "People had to stay in one place long enough to cultivate the barley—"

"—that was watered," Chip interrupted as if chanting a psalm, "by Ninkasi." He was referring to a Sumerian hymn, nearly four thousand years old, sung to the goddess of beer. The song is famous among homebrew nerds like us since, in the process of praising the divine, it details the production of beer: from fermenting the malt and cooling the mash to filtering the beer. "Ninkasi, it is you who pour out the filtered beer of the collector vat; it is like the onrush of the Tigris and the Euphrates."[1] Such praise makes it the earliest known beer recipe, not to mention one of the earliest hymns, on record.

Another drink. The fire popped hard, throwing embers into some dry leaves and we both got up to make sure they were stamped out.

"Maybe fire's the root of civilization," I remembered out loud.

"Prometheus right?" Chip offered.

"Yep, stole fire from the Gods and gave it to mortals."

1. Black, et al., "Hymn to Ninkasi," lines 45–48.

"Good thing 'cause it's gettin' chilly."

"Good thing."

So, we toasted the Titan.

∞

In the Greek language, "Prometheus" means *forethought* or *thinking ahead*, and even today the term *Promethean* is often used as a way of talking about creativity and innovation, as if our imaginations were being stoked or fired up. "In one short word, then, learn the truth condensed," declares the ancient playwright Aeschylus, "All arts of mortals from Prometheus spring."[2]

For anyone interested in the origins of knowing, the arrival of stone tools over 2.5 million years ago is as good example as any for one of these fired up moments in our ancestral origins, a marker in the origins of the human mind and culture. It would be a stretch to call tool-making the root of civilization—an imprecise and dubious term anyway[3]—but it does represent a new kind of relationship with the environment and with the world of forged objects. It is a relationship that outlasts the species that invented the practice of tool-making itself and one that eventually leads to a species that is so entangled with its cultural products that life is unimaginable without them.

We cannot know to what extent, if any, these early tool-makers were actually thinking ahead, but perhaps hiding out in that social attentiveness and imitative learning were some seeds of forethought, later to be cracked wide open by the fires of the Greek god.

Hominids and Hand Axes

On a timeline covering the last seven million years, you would find the rise of at least a dozen or more species of hominids—those descending from that ancestor we share with chimpanzees and bonobos. If you were to zoom in on the section of timeline between two million and one million years

2. Aeschylus. *Prometheus Bound*, lines 546–47.

3. In the end, the term *civilization* is too slippery for anything but late-night beer-inspired conversations. While it does suggest a certain complexity of culture going on among a group of people, the term is often loaded with prejudices that tend to underestimate the complexity of cultures other than one's own.

ago, you could find a half dozen or more of these hominid species overlapping one another to various degrees and all living on the continent of Africa.[4] Most, if not all, of them are descendents of Lucy. However, in this same period between two and one million years ago, all the *Australopithecines* disappear. So do those hominids named for tool use, *Homo habilis*, even as the Olduwan style of tool-making endures.

As far as anyone can tell today, one million years ago only one hominid species remained on earth, the one with the largest body up to that point. It had the largest brain as well. That species was *Homo erectus*, the "upright human."[5] This ancestor liked to move. *Homo erectus* was the first to travel off the continent of Africa, and did so as early as 1.7 million years ago. The bones of *Homo erectus* have been found not only in Africa, but in China and Indonesia as well as in the Republic of Georgia (on the threshold of Europe). In fact, this hominid traveler managed to survive in and out of Africa for hundreds of thousands of years, perhaps living as recently as 50 thousand years ago in Indonesia.[6]

With the fossils of *Homo erectus* we also find the first real innovation in relation to the production and style of stone tools. Alongside the more rugged Olduwan chopper, which continues to be made, a more sophisticated hand axe begins appearing in the fossil record approximately 1.5 million years ago (see picture on page 50). The axe has been dubbed the Acheulean style of tool-making, named for an area of France (near Saint-Acheul) where an excavation uncovered some of the earliest examples in the nineteenth century. The nomenclature can be confusing. The tools take their name from France, where they were first found, but since then the tools have been discovered throughout Africa, predating those in France. In other words, African hominids took the tools and style with them as they began to travel.[7]

4. These species of hominid are: *Homo habilis, Homo erectus, Homo rudolfensis, Homo ergaster, Australopithecus robustus,* and *Australopithecus boisei* (also known as *Paranthropus robustus* and *Paranthropus boisei*).

5. Until recently it was believed that *Homo erectus* was a direct descendent of *Homo habilis*, perhaps with *Homo ergaster* in between. However, many debate whether or not *ergaster* was simply another form of *erectus*; in addition, recent finds are making it look as if *erectus* and *habilis* existed alongside each other, sharing some common relative between two and three million years ago.

6. Swisher and Rink, "*Homo erectus* of Java."

7. The issue is a large one since there still tends to be a European bias in discussions of human evolution. Because innovations in tool styles, artifacts, and cave paintings, for example, were first discovered in Europe (where there were more resources to do the

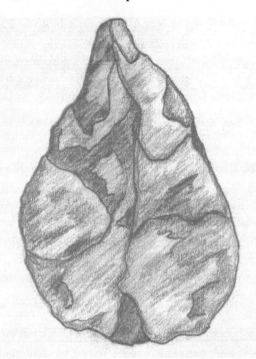

When comparing Olduwan tool-making to not making tools at all, the results are quite impressive. As mentioned in the last chapter, other animals may make tools of one sort or another, but even our closest primate cousins—chimps and bonobos—seem unable to master the art of producing simple Olduwan-style cores and flakes. Not only in the wild, but those in captivity who have been shown and enticed and trained for years cannot pull it off. While the manual dexterity seems to be available to them (some have learned to tie shoelaces for example), grasping the angles and the appropriate amount of force, along with the attention span such "knapping" requires, so far have eluded even the most teachable nonhuman primates.[8]

Even so, when Olduwan tools are compared to this emerging Acheulean teardrop style, the older tools look like little more than broken rocks. Whether viewed from the side, in profile, or viewed face on, front or back, Acheulean hand axes were hammered out to create a symmetrical shape, a

work in the first place), a false picture began to emerge. That is, while human anatomy may have evolved on the continent of Africa, it was still assumed (falsely) that the human mind and culture evolved in Europe. See Mcrearty and Brooks, "Revolution."

8. Mithen, *Prehistory*, 96–97; Greenspan and Shanker, *First Idea*, 146. Calvin, *Brief History*, 41.

result that is not particularly easy to accomplish. While the older choppers could be created with a couple of good collisions with a larger rock, the new hand axe would have taken much more time to craft and would have required even greater precision and dexterity. The edges and breaks on the older choppers appear relatively random—the makers being satisfied with creating any sharp edge on the core. But the stone axe makers do not appear to be so easily satisfied; they are interested in form.

Research among those, now, who try to recreate these ancient axes shows that there is a lot of contingency in producing them. Each rock will "have its own unique characteristics and challenges," as Steven Mithen puts it, due to the unpredictability of each fracture. That is, "to produce standardized forms the knapper needs to exploit and adapt his or her tool-making knowledge, rather than just follow a fixed set of rules in a rote fashion."[9]

Even so, even with this creative moment in prehistory, the age of imitation is not over. Acheulean tool-making is certainly more sophisticated than anything before, but this style, like the Olduwan before, lasts another million years without seeing major changes.[10] Again, imitation dominates over innovation. Yet, here, the imitation is more fine-tuned, including a more precise imitation of the product itself, not simply the behavior. With the Acheulean style of axe, the form of the product itself receives much more attention. In a sense, it would seem that the keen attention to the behavior of others (which allows us to imitate in the first place) is here supplemented with keen attention to the form rock can take if chipped in a certain way. This would be imitation extended, so to speak, helping the form of one rock to imitate the form of another rock. The tool-maker stands in between.

In all, the increased degree of difficulty, when combined with the necessary attention, dexterity, and capacity to deal with contingencies, does seem to point to some new mental and physical skills coming into play with *Homo erectus*. To be sure, these bigger, traveling tool-makers had style.

Back to the Fire

With new wood on the fire, Chip and I were granted a light show. Flames danced, accompanied by more pops and cracks from the moisture escaping the maple. My gaze fixed upon a dazzling array of colors revealing themselves—so many shades of yellows and oranges and blues appearing

9. Mithen, *Prehistory*, 118–19, 242.
10. Calvin, *Brief History*, 41.

then hiding again, flowing and floating until I was half dizzy with the
...ty of it. I began to wonder. Did early tool-makers ever delight in their
work? Did seeds of pride sprout even a little—any sense of accomplishment
when one of our million-year-old ancestors completed a fine stone axe?
Would the crafter hold it up for others to see, as a child holds up a drawing
to a parent? Sometimes I wonder: if not then—when?

∞

The reason I wondered—why I continue to wonder—is that other primates
don't. They don't point or gesture to get their fellows to look at other objects
at all. Not in the wild anyway. They don't hold up sticks or food or babies
or point to a great new tree or watering hole or termite mound to show
others, to show off, or in any other way invite the attention of others to
anything beyond themselves. Not even for the benefit of mates or offspring.
Only humans do these, engage in what cognitive psychologists call joint or
shared attention.[11]

As Michael Tomasello describes joint attention in his book about human cognition, six-month-old human babies will engage with other people
and with objects in a dyadic way—one to one. If a baby is interacting with
an object, say a rattle, they tend to ignore Mom or Dad or anyone else. If
someone gets the baby's attention and begins interacting with her, then she
is likely to ignore the rattle. But for most children, a little miracle occurs
somewhere between nine months of age and a year. Children begin to share
attention with others. "Most prototypically," in Tomasello's words, "it is at
this age that infants for the first time begin to flexibly and reliably look
where adults are looking (gaze following), to engage with them in relatively
extended bouts of social interaction mediated by an object (joint engagement), to use adults as social reference points (social referencing), and to
act on objects in the way adults are acting on them (imitative learning)."[12]
This is the point in the child's life that he will begin to point, to hold up
or show something to others. And all this begins before most of us can
remember anything at all, so we cannot even imagine life in any other way.

11. Tomasello *Cultural Origins*, 21. Some great apes raised in captivity will point or
reach for an object in the company of humans (e.g., to food that is out of reach), suggesting the seeds of joint attention. See also Leavens and Hopkins, "Intentional Communication by Chimpanzees." A fuller discussion of gestures in primates will come in ch. 13.

12. Tomasello *Cultural Origins*, 62. The exception—one Tomasello discusses—is
among children with autism.

Human culture, as we know it, would not be possible without these little triangles of interaction, this sharing.

Perhaps our bonobo brothers and chimpanzee sisters feel something like pride, but for humans today the feeling tends to be all wrapped up in this ability to share attention with others. And it is at least possible that the origins of this new form of tool that emerges a million and a half years ago, this elegant little hand axe, is all wrapped up in the ability to hold it up for others to behold. Perhaps such a shared gaze is necessary to create such a tool with such a particular form in the first place. Or maybe not. Perhaps this evolution of human attention takes even longer to come about.

We can wonder.

Ancient Fires

What about fire itself?

Whether prompted by campfires and beer or not, there are good and intriguing reasons for looking into the fire for the unseen powers at work in human thinking. To the ancient Greek imagination, not only fire, but thought itself was a gift stolen from the gods: "Before as babes / By me [Prometheus] were roused to reason, taught to think."[13] What kind of thought would it take to create a fire? What kind of forethought? Or perhaps it is the case that, as a good campfire between friends can do, fire invites shared attention?

Until very recently, the oldest reliable evidence for controlled fire was about 250 thousand years old. But that has changed. A research team headed up by Professor Naama Goren-Inbar of the Hebrew University of Jerusalem has produced evidence that could push this dating back over a half million years, squarely in the Acheulian era of stone tool-making. The team has been painstakingly excavating a bog in Israel called Gesher Benot Ya'aqov, what was once an ancient lakeshore, with its remains dating to 790 thousand years ago.[14] They have been sorting through thousands and thousands of pieces of flint, wood, and seeds—preserved because of the lack of oxygen in the bog.

What the team has found is that a small percentage of these remains show signs of being burnt (less than 2 percent of the wood and flint). But the important factor is that the remains showing evidence of burning were

13. Aeschylus. *Prometheus Bound*, lines 483–84.
14. Goren-Inbar, et al., "Fire."

clustered together in a couple different locations, suggesting hearths, that is, controlled, intentional burning. The reason that a small percentage of burning is so suggestive is that it helps rule out the possibility that wildfire or volcanic fire was the cause of the burning. If naturally occurring fires were the cause, everything would show signs of burning, and many of the specimens would not even exist since such natural fires burn so much hotter.

In a report of their findings in the journal *Science*, the researchers say the evidence suggests that the inhabitants of this site "hunted, processed meat, extracted marrow, quarried and transported different kinds of rock, produced stone tools, gathered plant foods, and produced fire." They go on to conclude, "On the basis of all the GBY archaeological data, we suggest that the hominins who frequented the shores of the lake for over 100 thousand years knew how to use fire and exercised that knowledge repeatedly throughout much of the Acheulian cultural period. The domestication of fire by hominins surely led to dramatic changes in behavior connected with diet, defense, and social interaction."[15] At a minimum fire would have been a great ally in the chilly nights and seasons these hominids were discovering as they traveled abroad to cooler climates.

But who were those fire-building ancestors living along a Middle Eastern lakeshore nearly 800 thousand years ago? So far, nobody knows. Recall that one million years ago the only remaining hominid on earth was *Homo erectus*, with whom the Acheulean style of tool-making is associated. Over the next few hundred thousand years, however, the fossil record shows signs of new spinoffs—hominids who share many features of *erectus*, but also show a few features of more recent species. Goren-Inbar suggests it is possible that the residents of this site could have been *Homo ergaster*, for example, or "archaic" *Homo sapiens*, both of which could fall into this territory between *erectus* and our own species of *Homo sapiens*.[16] So far there has not been enough evidence to say for sure.[17]

15. Ibid., 727.

16. Ibid. The term *archaic* is simply a way of describing species that fall in between *Homo erectus* and *Homo sapiens*. Scholars debate whether or not these in-between types should really be considered new species or still be called *Homo erectus*.

17. As this book was being prepared for press, evidence of even earlier controlled fire—one million years ago—among *Homo erectus* was published, based upon materials from the Wonderwerk Cave, Northern Cape province, South Africa. See Berna et al., "Microstratigraphic."

Paleoanthropologists do know that by 500 thousand years ago a new species had spun off of from *Homo erectus* in Africa, sometimes called *Homo heidelbergensis*. This name (like so many of the others) is also a bit confusing because even though it appears to have arisen in Africa, it was first discovered in Germany, and so named.

Like *Homo erectus, heidelbergensis* lived both on and off the continent of Africa and is particularly important to the story of human origins since it gave rise to two other species—the Neanderthals and us. The Neanderthals evolved off the continent of Africa, living in Europe and Western Asia, existing from about 250 thousand to 30 thousand years ago. *Homo sapiens* appear to have spun off from *heidelbergensis* as well, only they did so solely in Africa. Currently the best candidates for the earliest *Homo sapiens* fossils come from Ethiopia and date somewhere between 160 thousand and 200 thousand years ago.[18]

There is also the possibility of another line of hominids descending from *Homo erectus* in Indonesia, based upon fossils from the island of Flores—*Homo floresiensis*—the so-called hobbit, because these hominids were only about three feet tall.[19] The implications of this remarkable 2003 discovery are still being debated, but the dating of these fossils suggest that *floresiensis* lived until as recently as 18 thousand years ago, far outlasting the Neanderthals, and representing their own unique line from *Homo erectus.*[20]

So, to summarize these moments of a complicated history that I have already oversimplified, one million years ago one hominid species remained—*Homo erectus* in Africa. By 150 thousand years ago,[21] two descendant species remained—the Neanderthals out of Africa and we *Homo sapiens* in Africa. *Homo erectus* likely survived in Indonesia until 50 thousand years ago, also possibly giving rise to *Homo floresiensis*, who lived until as recent as 18 thousand years ago.

As it turns out, *Homo sapiens* end up being quite the travelers as well. Some 100 thousand years ago, they thrived throughout Africa and spread to the adjacent Levant. By 60 thousand years ago they made it to Australia and by 40 thousand years ago they joined the Neanderthals in Europe (and possibly *erectus* and *floresiensis* in Indonesia). So far there is no clear evidence

18. Concerning the dating of these fossils, see McDougall et al., "Modern Humans."

19. Brown et al., "New Small-Bodied Hominin."

20. For another view of *H. florensiensis*, see Wong, "Rethinking the Hobbit," who suggests the possibility that the species could have evolved from another older than *erectus.*

21. Probably closer to 200 thousand years ago.

for interbreeding between the Neanderthals (or *erectus* or *floresiensis*) and *Homo sapiens*, and experts debate whether this would have been biologically possible. So the Neanderthals, the hobbits, and *Homo erectus* go the route of all the other species of hominids before: they die out.

Homo sapiens are the last of the line, so far, that began some six or seven million years ago. Whether or not there could be another spinoff from us a million years from now, who knows? We could, like so many species before us, be a dead end.

Cooler Thoughts

"So how long you think we'll make it?" I asked Chip, breaking the silence. The fire had burned down and cooler thoughts were emerging, as they inevitably do, crowding out the wonder that had earlier attended the flames. I cannot say for sure whether forethought or reason or thinking itself smothers wonder, but I too have eaten from the know-it-all tree and can at such moments feel the curse of foresight.

"What do you mean?" Chip asked.

"Humans—how long you think we'll survive? Lucy's people made it at least a million years, we're not even close, maybe a couple hundred thousand."

"Damn." He paused to think about it. "I don't know."

"Me neither." And Frankenstein jumped into my mind.

I was remembering that Mary Shelly's tale of Dr. Frankenstein and his monster is subtitled *The Modern Prometheus*. Dr. Frankenstein steals the spark of life from the heavens and, in doing so, creates a trail of death and heartache in its wake. This story too, with echoes of that first case of overreaching in the garden of Eden, represents a kind of parable warning its hearers of the dangers of unleashing the power of Prometheus. Fire creates, fire destroys. Our climb up the ladder of knowing is loaded with perils not only for ourselves but for the planet; perhaps the gods have been trying to warn us all along. Prometheus, after all, was punished by Zeus for his crime—chained to a mountain side with an eagle perpetually tearing his body and feasting on his liver.

Homo sapiens have "come far up the heat ladder," observed Loren Eiseley six decades ago, so far that the naturalist turns moralist, if not apocalyptic, in his reflections upon the journey. The species has become like a long-armed crab manipulating "tongs in dangerous atomic furnaces." How far up the ladder can we climb? "Before this century is out, either *duplex* must learn that knowledge without greatness of spirit is not for man, or there will remain only his calcined cities and the little charcoal of his bones." To call us *Homo duplex* is to draw upon an old theological tradition—we are creatures partaking of evil and good alike. Both struggle within us perpetually. And though we have made it into a new century, I find it difficult to argue with the substance of his warning. Humanity itself is "a flame—a great roaring, wasteful furnace devouring irreplaceable substances of the earth."[22]

The greatness of spirit necessary to survive as a species and not burn up the rest, now, may require another incarnation of Promethean foresight, that is, the vision to look ahead and temper our fiery appetites. For Eiseley the ability to do so is fundamentally tied to our ways of seeing and knowing the world around us. The great temptation fueling the fires seems to flow from the very mind that can climb the ladder and see so much from such a high view. The climb breeds a certain cold-hearted reductionism that is "so busy stripping things apart that . . . the only true reality becomes the chill void of ever-streaming particles." In such a cold atmosphere, wonder and compassion die. "One can only assert that in science, as in religion, when one has destroyed human wonder and compassion, one has killed man, even if the man in question continues to go about his laboratory tasks."[23]

The greatness of spirit, then, grows in the ground of awe, "a controlled sense of wonder before the universal mystery, whether it hides in a snail's eye or within the light that impinges on that delicate organ."[24] Loren Eiseley could see this wonder at work in the writings of a doubting Darwin and a believing Kierkegaard alike, in Einstein and Pascal, in cave paintings and modern classrooms. It is neither a matter of scientific principle nor theological creed, because, uprooted from wonder, even the best principles and creeds turn cold-hearted.

Wonder recognizes that the rivers of life run deeper than we can fully imagine, that there is ever more than meets the eye. Yet, knowing this, everything meeting our eyes becomes all the more meaningful.

22. Eiseley, *Star Thrower*, 51–52.
23. Ibid., 198.
24. Ibid., 190.

∞

"Time to call it a night." The fire was about out and it was late.
"Yep." We both got up and I started to walk home.
"Peace brother."
"Peace."

7

A Little Speculation

THE GREAT CHILD PSYCHIATRIST Robert Coles made a striking discovery while interviewing children for his book *The Spiritual Life of Children*. When among Christian children he would ask them to draw a picture of God. Out of nearly 300, all but 38 of these drawings were of God's face, "with maybe a neck, some shoulders, but no torso, arms, or legs"—just the face.[1] The face, his research would imply, holds intense meaning in human life, given that it so easily becomes an image of God for these children. And as strange as it may seem, and no doubt speculative, I have found myself thinking a lot about Coles's findings when pondering the intelligence at work in the lives of our tool-making ancestors over two million years ago. In a roundabout way there may be relationship.

In *The Spiritual Life of Children* Coles is obviously exploring theological territory as he meets and talks with children; he nonetheless never strays too far away from his own discipline of psychiatry. Trained by Anna Freud in fact, he not only searches for religious implications of so many drawings, he is ever curious about the psychological soil in which the face could be so meaningful. "Working with children over the years has taught me," writes Coles, "that they are quick to connect themselves, in all sorts of ways, to whatever it is they do. Picturing God's face turns out to be no exception. A child's race, class, sex, family experience, and idiosyncratic personal experience may work their way into the drawing he or she does,

---

1. Coles, *Spiritual Life*, 40. These were children who grew up with images of Jesus and the Creator from illustrated Bibles, Sunday school materials, or stained glass windows. See ch. 3, "The Face of God." He did not ask Jewish or Muslim children to draw God in light of stronger prohibitions against doing so.

though such influences contend with religious and cultural conventions that have exerted their own hold on the child."

From a psychological perspective, the face would seem to reflect both the everyday imaginations of these children as well as their best expression of the sacred they can muster: "faces full of so much authority, or grandeur, or power, or love, or mystery, or judgmental passion, or insight, or alarm, or worries, or vulnerability."[2]

Smiling Faces

Coles was far from the first in the world of psychology to point to the power of the face in the life of children. One of the most revealing investigations in this territory came decades earlier, in the 1930s and 40s, when research with children was still itself in its infancy. The team of René Spitz and Katherine Wolf attempted to trace out key developmental moments in the first year of life and along the way found themselves giving a lot of attention to faces—particularly smiling faces. They wanted to know when babies start smiling, and for whom or what.

Working with babies from varied ethnic and economic backgrounds as well as home situations, Spitz and Wolf found that, in general, infants do not smile before two months of age (only three of 145 children did). But more and more, between the ages of two and six months, they found that almost all the remaining babies began to smile (only three did not smile by six months). Along the way of the study, the researchers began to experiment with various stimuli for smiling in this age group. What or who makes a baby smile?

The short answer: the face. The human face nearly always generated a smile. Significantly, it did not matter whose face was presented to the young children—a parent, Spitz or Wolf, a stranger—as long as it was the full face. Frowning or smiling did not matter, but turning a profile or covering the experimenter's eyes would stop the smiling in the child. It did not even need to be a real face—a mask or a dummy was good enough, as long as it was about the same size as an adult human face, and as long as it was moved around a bit. A motionless mask would draw the gaze, but not the smile.

Spitz interpreted this finding as evidence of how the human face functions as the primary psychological organizer of a child's budding personhood. That is, by two months of age, the face "becomes a privileged visual

2. Ibid., 66–67.

percept, preferred to all other 'things' of the infant's environment." A child invests this preferred percept with "complete and prolonged attention."[3] So, long before babies can toddle or even stand up, before they can use a spoon or digest solid food or use words, these youngest members of our own species are so cued into the face of the other that they can only stare and smile.

By six months however, matters change. As the children Spitz and Wolfe worked with entered the second half of their first year of life, they became more discriminating: they would no longer smile for strangers, and frowns and dummies would no longer do. Children by this age would also try to imitate the familiar face—trying to purse lips or widen the mouth, for example, if the adult did so.[4] Full-blown and more obvious types of imitation appear more and more by 8 to 10 months—gestures, rolling a ball, hand movements, and the like.[5]

Generally then, in the first half of the first year of life comes the emergence of indiscriminate attention to, and smiling for, the face of another. In the second half comes more discriminating attention and smiling, as well as the ability to imitate. A developmental psychologist would say that imitation builds upon the interpersonal platform represented in these earliest smiling encounters, that the cognitive ability to imitate flows from a quality of attention established face to face.

Making Tools

So what do smiling faces have to do with tool-making hominids?

As the last chapter noted, the Olduwan and Acheulean styles of tool-making each lasted relatively unchanged for a million years. If Michael Tomasello and others are on the right track, the key kind of knowing that stands out in this industry of early hominid tool-making is a kind of social intelligence, a deep attunement to those faces and gazes and smiles and frowns that orient our attention and, if Spitz is correct, serve to organize our budding personalities in the first year of life. As Tomasello summarizes, "We may or may not be smarter than apes, but we are definitely more social."[6] Even more striking than the inventive australopithecine who first

3. Spitz, *First Year*, 86.

4. Ibid., 178.

5. See also Piaget, *Six Studies*, 19. In addition see Loder, *Transforming Moment*, ch. 6, for his use of the Spitz and Wolf study in a theological context.

6. Tomasello, "How Are Humans Unique?," 15.

chipped a flake off a core to initiate the Stone Age, was the way in which her fellows followed suit, paid sufficient attention to the act itself, which in turn allowed the tradition to continue to be copied generation after generation for a million years.

The wonderful question for speculation is why. Why would such a sharp interpersonal awareness have developed among hominid primates in the first place? What kinds of behaviors or ways of living or environmental situations could have nudged us, over time, toward keying in more and more to the activities of others? What kind of evolutionary payoff could there have been for such attention to our own kind, even to the detriment of more efficient and direct problem-solving techniques, if human two-year-olds with rakes are any clue?

One line of thought about this comes from William Calvin, and coincides with his notion of a "triple startup" (of tools, ice, and bigger brains) between two and three million years ago, when hominids began to eat meat as well. Calvin raises the possibility that in this new era of hunting or scavenging another skill may have developed, one with some evolutionary payoff. That skill is sharing.

As tools made eating meat more feasible for these formerly vegetarian primates, cooperation and sharing—especially in relation to food—could have been a very useful skill for surviving. As Calvin puts it, "even if a lone hunter kills a large antelope, it is too much meat for even a single family. The obvious strategy is to give most of it away and count on reciprocity tomorrow." He goes on to suggest that it may have begun simply as "tolerated scrounging," that is, you and I tolerate each other working off the same carcass. But such toleration may have eventually developed "into more elaborate forms of reciprocal altruism."[7] In other words sharing could yield strong rewards—food and survival for instance—for the groups of hominids that practiced it, in turn honing the social attentiveness necessary to imitation. Scavenging meat, chopping open or scraping bones with sharp rocks, tolerated scrounging, and a bit of sharing could have all mutually reinforced each other to heighten hominid attentiveness to one another.

Closely related, Stanley Greenspan and Stuart Shanker, authors of *The First Idea*, wonder whether the cognitive ability to make a tool in the first place may have been more the fruit of a social intelligence than the cause. Specifically, they point to the critical ability of paying attention. Whether attending to the stones being knapped and the physics involved (force and

7. Calvin, *Brief History*, 39.

angles) or attending to the ones carrying out the practice, it would take a high level of attention to craft stones into tools, let alone to sustain the tradition for a million years. And despite some signs of promise among domesticated apes, Greenspan and Shanker point out that "great apes in the wild seldom appear to engage in interactions for more than a few seconds at a time."[8]

This takes us back to those smiling faces. Shanker and Greenspan see the roots of the cognitive and attentional abilities to craft stone tools over two million years ago in caregiving. Parenting. Specifically, they believe the emotional signaling and expressions going on in those face-to-face interactions between a caregiver and a child are the key to the originality of the human mind as well as to the social stability and cohesiveness necessary to pass along cultural practices from one generation to another. As Shanker and Greenspan describe them, emotionally rich, caring practices of nurture "enabled these early humans to establish deeper feelings of engagement: to engage in longer exchanges, to understand one another better, and to develop more complex relationships."[9] Deeper levels of attachment, and for longer periods, would yield many fruits—including greater social cohesion (perhaps leading to forms of sharing, for example) and even greater attention spans (of the sort that could focus long enough to make tools, for example).

This focus upon nurturing practices makes even more sense when considering that such behaviors as tolerated scrounging or sharing or even more elaborate forms of reciprocal altruism, whenever they did appear, did not likely do so whole cloth from nowhere. They could easily have been an expansion of behaviors already in play for the task of taking care of children. Hominid children then, as now, would have been highly dependent upon caretaking parents if they were to survive. To a degree this is true of all primates, as well as mammals generally.

As Susan Allport explains in her book *A Natural History of Parenting*, different species over time have developed a wide variety of behaviors for ensuring the survival of another generation of the species. Some—like most fish, reptiles, and insects—survive through numbers. Massive quantities of offspring are produced. For example, eels lay millions of eggs every season, but most of these will not make it; they will be killed off early by predators and climate. But enough do make it to keep the species going. As she puts

8. Greenspan and Shanker, *First Idea*, 146.
9. Ibid., 144.

it, "Beyond producing good sized eggs and finding, perhaps, a suitable spot to lay them, most animal parents never even see their young. And were they to see them, they would be much more inclined to eat them than to offer them food, protection, or guidance."[10] Other species, most birds, for example, and some mammals such as rats and mice, use nesting systems. That is, they hide and shelter a smaller number of offspring and tend to them—as long as they are in the nest. Among the nesters, "the parents need never even learn to recognize them as individuals, or vice versa. They certainly don't need to become attached to one another."[11] Proper caretaking for the species, good parenting of the offspring, in these circumstances does not require knowing who the children are, let alone bonding with them with anything like the love humans feel for their young.

But for many mammals, including primates, recognition and attachment are critical to survival and to the social structures of the species. Various kinds of surveillance systems help parent and offspring stick close to each other for protection and nourishment. And this returns us again to faces. As Allport describes the situation in a chapter entitled "The Evolution of Love," "Attachment is maintained by a host of reciprocal signals that change over time, allowing for more and more exploration and independence. The signals vary with the animal: monkey infants cling; human infants cry, smile, gaze, and, later follow; ducklings pipe; and lambs bleat."[12]

In all, the more dependent we are initially on that face of another for sheer survival, and the longer this is the case, the more attentive to others we would likely become as a species. The situation could be intensified as hominids were learning how to wander more and more out of the protection of dense forests and into open savannahs, for example, to find food.

And so it is for such reasons as these that Greenspan and Shanker see faces and smiles so intertwined with tool-making and caretaking. As hominid brains got larger (especially with *Homo habilis*) more development occurred outside the womb and the period of dependence upon caregivers became even longer. In turn, this could have led to longer and deeper levels of attachment. Faces and smiles lead to attachment, attention, imitation, social cohesion and stability, and perhaps eventually to reciprocal altruism, allowing tool-making to endure.

10. Allport, *Parenting*, 14.
11. Ibid., 169.
12. Ibid., 170.

In this odd kind of way, hominid tool-making is all tangled up with love.

It is a theory, anyway, and a fascinating one from the point of view parenting, learning, and child development. Greenspan, in particular, is a leading expert in the area of autism and related issues, and works intensively with parents of children who, due to biological factors, in fact have difficulty picking up the social cues and intentions of others, and therefore have difficulty with the wake of cultural skills and knowledge that follow. So he sees firsthand the power and importance of these long exchanges of social interaction, imitation, and emotional signaling—how interrelated they are, and how difficult learning the ways of a family, a community, and a culture are when they do not come so easily to a child.

However, in the end we cannot know for sure whether we can read back onto those first tool-makers what seems to be so true now. And that is why such a discussion is particularly speculative. It is not difficult to imagine a reversed scenario, that is, that the kind of attentiveness required to craft a stone tool could have enhanced attentiveness to a child, in turn allowing longer periods of brain development outside the womb. Tool-making and tolerated scrounging, in this scenario, could have led the way to more intense social engagement with children rather than the other way around.

Things Seen and Unseen

So, which behaviors led to what kinds of knowing 2.6 million years ago is hard to say, and may always be impossible to determine with certainty. But at the least we can notice a powerful convergence of several factors and dynamics at this point in the hominid story: ice, tools, scrape marks on animal bones, a new hominid (*habilis*), and bigger brains. These are some of the traces, the visible elements, that allow us to speculate about life among our ancestors so long ago.

But as you can see, these visible items have led to a list of possible invisible behaviors and developments that, with caution, we might add: imitative learning, enhanced social intelligence, longer durations of attention, deeper attachment, complex nurturing practices, tolerated scrounging, an intuitive physics, and finer-grained hand dexterity. All these invisibles can only be known indirectly from things visible—and that too may tell us something about ourselves as original knowers. The tree of knowledge reveals worlds seen and unseen alike. And speculation itself is born of our ability to know things invisible, to infer powers at work in the world from their fruits, whether in the physical environment, in other people, or in ourselves even—forces and dynamics no one can ever see directly.

It may be no accident that the children studied by Robert Coles turned to the visible face to depict an invisible God. From a biblical perspective they are in good company. The face is a frequent and powerful image permeating Jewish and Christian scriptures, often used to symbolize God's presence or relationship to humanity, as in the blessing from Psalm 31: "Let your face shine upon your servant; save me in your steadfast love" (v. 16). In this case the face is equivalent to God's enduring love, a theme picked up and extended by the apostle Paul in the Christian New Testament: "When I was a child, I spoke like a child, I thought like a child, I reasoned like a child; when I became an adult, I put an end to childish ways. For now we see in a mirror, dimly, but then we will see face to face. Now I know only in part; then I will know fully, even as I have been fully known. And now faith, hope, and love abide, these three; and the greatest of these is love" (1 Cor 13:11–12). Theologically speaking, the face is an expression of God's presence, God's attachment, God's affection.[13] And in the case of Paul's letter, seeing face to face is all tied in with maturity and wisdom, with knowing, with knowing what ultimately matters. The face is all tied up with love.

In the end, the extent to which smiling infants in the 1940s or the theological drawings of children can reveal something about Stone Age hominids or the other way around is ultimately unclear, but they do all seem to suggest that a certain kind of interpersonal awareness could be critical to who we are, to the building blocks of human thought and culture, and even to the importance of matters of the heart for matters of the human mind. Infants—now at least—are primed and ready to smile in the presence of the face. We are wonderfully made to notice, to smile at, to delight in, and to thrive on the sheer presence of another. We are born to attach, to stick with others, and perhaps herein lies the foundation for something as basic as a little tolerated scrounging, if not the out-and-out sharing.

ck out us-them research

---

13. Wigger, *Texture*, 145–46; and Wigger, "Facing," provide fuller discussions of these points.

∞

Coles ends his discussion of "The Face of God" (ch. 3) in *The Spiritual Life of Children* by reflecting upon his days of working in the soup kitchens with the great social justice advocate Dorothy Day. One afternoon in particular, he recounts, several of the volunteers had struggled with what they called in those days a "Bowery bum." Coles describes him as "an angry, cursing, truculent man of 50 or so, with long gray hair, a full, scraggly beard, a huge scar on his right cheek, a mouth with virtually no teeth, and bloodshot eyes, one of which had a terrible tic." Coles remembers what Day told them: "For all we know he might be God Himself come here to test us, so let us treat him as an honored guest and look at his face as if it is the most beautiful one we can imagine."[14]

As many of us would, Coles found this difficult. At the time, Coles was focused upon things visible, in a sense taking the text of this man's face a little too literally perhaps, and forgetting that we always see only in part. Yet to be human, whether a psychiatrist looking into the soulful drawings of children or an advocate looking into the sorrowful eyes of a hungry fellow, to be human is to know there is more.

14. Coles, *Spiritual Life*, 67.

8

Monarchs and the Mousterian Mind

LAST WEEK I SAW a monarch butterfly. It was dipping and dodging about the edges of my all-but-faded garden, probably looking for some zinnia nectar to feed upon or a milkweed plant for laying eggs. The sight of these royal insects never fails to inspire me, not only for their beauty and grace, but for the immense journey they make every fall, and again every spring. Each year as the weather warms, they will find their way from Mexico, through the States, and on up into fields and forests of Canada. Then at the end of the summer and into the fall, they reverse the trip all the way back to the same area where they started.

As part of a family that makes its own regular migration to the Canadian wilderness, I am amazed by something else: a butterfly's sense of direction. I hate to admit how many times we have gotten lost—both on the roadways heading north as well as among the lakes and woods we fish. We have overshot so many highways and gravel roads, have missed so many trailheads and portage routes, and found ourselves on the wrong lakes with such frequency that I don't really know why we didn't give up a long time ago.

One particularly illustrative occasion: we got up early to get a good start on the day, but maybe too early as a fog had rolled in on the lake over night. We knew the route so well, a straight shot across the lake, that all we had to do was aim the boat in the right direction and with our little six-horse outboard motor we would hit the other shore in 10 to 15 minutes. Even if we were off a bit, we could follow the shore to the trailhead, and by the time we would portage everything over to the next, much larger lake the fog would have burned off so we could continue the journey. That was our thinking.

So we took off slowly, making sure we had lined ourselves up well to hit our target. Given the lack of visibility, we went slower than usual to be careful. But the water is deep all the way, so there was no real danger of hitting anything. So we didn't think too much of it when 20 minutes later, even 25, there was still no sign of the shore. At 30 minutes we wondered why we never thought to bring a compass, and we were baffled. No shore. So we adjusted direction just a tad, figuring the slight breeze must have put us at more of an angle than we realized. Still, 45 minutes later, no shore.

As it turns out, we were right about one thing. The fog began to lift after about an hour, and soon, coming into view, finally, was the shore. We began to make out other boats, and a dock, and familiar landmarks, and the clearer they became the clearer the truth of what had happened became. These were all the things that should not be at the portage—we had made one huge, blind circle and were back where we had started.

Butterflies amaze me.

Still, it is a little misleading to portray monarchs going from Mexico to Canada and back every year. They do and they don't. That is, most monarchs only live four to five weeks, not long enough to make either the trip north or south. In the spring, as they begin migrating they engage in a kind of relay race, laying eggs along the way.[1] Each successive generation takes the family journey a little farther, both through time and through space, until several generations later something remarkable happens. In the fall, a special generation of monarchs, called the "Methuselah generation" is born, so named for the grandfather of Noah, who, Genesis says, lived to be 969 years old. These monarchs live seven to eight months, making the trip back home to Mexico—sometimes even to the same tree as their great-great-grandparents—and then they make the initial spring migration when the time is right.

So butterflies amaze me. They too make a big circle every year, but not by getting lost. Humans have to make maps and compasses and GPS systems to find their way. Monarchs fly. And they do so with all the power of tiny, paper-thin wings that will get blown about every which way before they arrive. Still, they know the way home.

---

1. The relay race analogy is from World Wildlife Fund, "Monarch of Migration."

Two Temptations

Along the way of trying to understand human knowing better, we almost inevitably find ourselves looking around the rest of creation and making comparisons. How are we different? How are we the same? The fact that we make such comparisons may even say more about our minds than what we find, especially given that there seem to be a couple of powerful pulls drawing our thoughts toward two different ends of a pole. Temptations really, ones I feel in myself when I consider other creatures.

On one end of the axis is the assumption that because animals do not write poetry or build space stations their intelligence is automatically inferior to that of humans. Perhaps this is the hubris of human knowing. If we think of intelligence along human standards and functions, maybe other creatures are less intelligent in some senses, but monarch butterflies give me pause.

The other, almost opposite, temptation is imagining that other creatures think a lot like we do. The closer to the human family we get—mammals, primates, chimps—or the more an animal is part of the human domesticated world—dogs, cats, horses—the more we imagine and talk about these creatures as if they have minds much like our own. Understandable because we value them, but nonetheless, this too can be a form of hubris as we still tie their creaturely worth to their ability to think like we do. In one direction we are drawn to our differences, in the other our similarities.

These temptations are also in play as we consider the ways of knowing in our hominid ancestors. Either they must have been less intelligent or they must have thought like we do. The fact is, we don't know. Either could be true; neither could be true. But I think it helps to know the temptations are there, even as we compare. Though the origins of human ways of knowing may be forever foggy, we do now and then seem to catch a glimpse of the shore. It could be that we are only going in a big circle, blindly projecting our assumptions back into the past, if not onto the universe itself. On the other hand, perhaps we too easily reserve greatness for *Homo sapiens* alone and their all-powerful minds.

Then again, perhaps with each generation we have the chance to contribute to the trip, handing off a bit of direction or a sense of home along the way, the way of this grand, colorful pilgrimage into life.

A Mind-Body Problem

So much has happened since the time when a community of hominids in the Middle East built a fire 790 thousand years ago. More travels, more species, more extinctions, maybe even more mind. By the time we hit the 50-thousand-years-ago mark, *Homo sapiens* have already been around for some 150 thousand years, and have spread around the continent of Africa and into Asia and Australia, and they are about ready to hit Europe. *Homo heidelbergensis* has come and gone; *Homo erectus* and *neanderthalensis* are on their way out, forever. The three-foot *Homo floresiensis* may still be thriving, but isolated to a couple of islands in Indonesia.

Some important anatomical changes occur on the way to becoming *Homo sapiens* as well, changes that in a roundabout way may even have a connection to the migratory skills of butterflies. These are changes in the bodies of humans that eventually have important consequences for our minds as well as our behaviors. For example, the larynx—the voice box—drops, creating more space in the throat, which in turn allows for a greater range of sounds. Teeth are getting smaller, which creates more and more room in the mouth to shape those sounds even as the nerves that control the tongue and our chest muscles for breathing become more fine-tuned.[2] Not only helpful for producing speech, but as William Calvin points out, these developments are good for "swimming, sustained running, and blowing at embers to keep the fire going."[3] To top it all off, brains are getting bigger, nearly twice the size from those a million years ago, four times the size as Lucy's three million years ago.

These changes raise a huge philosophical issue, one debated for millennia, often called the "mind-body problem." What is the relationship between the body and the mind? These days the most intense version of the question focuses specifically on the brain: what is the relationship between the mind and the brain?

Until now, I have been using the terms *mind* and *brain*, in an everyday language way, almost interchangeably. But when you think about it, matters are not so simple. The term *mind* is a particularly slippery notion, paradoxically enough, a mental construction. It is really more of an umbrella term referring to invisible ideas, thoughts, memories, beliefs, attitudes, consciousness, and in general all kinds of cognitive processes and

2. See Mithen, *Singing Neanderthal*, 146; and Calvin, *Brief History*, 56–57.
3. Calvin, *Brief History*, 57.

powers. *Brain* is a little more straightforward; at least it has been for the past few centuries since it has been studied. Brains can be seen (although, thank goodness, I've only seen pictures) and have physical limits. Who can say where the mind begins or ends? Nobody doubts there is a strong relationship between the two. For example, we know that disruptions in the brain—a blow to the head, Alzheimer's, hallucinogenic drugs, epilepsy—can create all kinds of havoc on the mental life, from forms of amnesia to the inability to read or speak. But to what extent is the reverse true? Can or to what extent does the invisible life of the mind affect the visible life of our big-brained bodies?

The pure physicality of the brain makes it much easier to study in many ways, including the ability to estimate its size in the past. Paleontologists can derive good estimates of brain size because there are physical skulls to work with. The mind, on the other hand, is not only invisible and hard to delimit; we have to infer its "size" and character indirectly from behaviors and practices—cultural artifacts and language, for example. Difficult enough in the present, maybe impossible for the past.

More on this mind-body, mind-brain issue will come later, but for now it is enough to notice that an evolutionary account of our hominid past has its own version of the ancient puzzle, one raising as many questions as ever. It starts with a body-body problem, or more precisely, a head-body problem. Between Lucy and modern humans, we got really big-headed.

Big-Headed

Like our brains, on average, the rest of our hominid bodies have been growing since Lucy, only not at the same rate. In fact, if our bodies had been growing at a comparable rate as our brains, we would be somewhere between 15 and 20 feet tall on average. This means that our EQ has been growing, the so-called *encephalization quotient*, which is the relationship between brain and body size. An EQ of 1.0 is the figure used to represent the average EQ of all mammals. Rodents come in at 0.5. In other words, their brains are about half the relative size of the mammal average. An average primate, at 2.0, is twice the average. Fish and reptiles measure in at 0.05, which is to say, at 1/20th the size of the average mammal, so their "brainpower" is significantly less than that of mammals.[4]

4. Zeman, *Consciousness*, 255ff. Zeman, a neurologist, provides an excellent summary of EQ and its relationship to what he intentionally describes as "brainpower" (instead of the term "intelligence").

Therefore, to say that the EQ of hominids has been growing over the years is to say that our brains have been getting larger and larger compared to the rest of our bodies. Three million years ago, Lucy and her fellow australopithecines had an EQ of about 3.4, slightly greater than chimps at 2.6, and less than half of the 7.0 of modern humans.[5] But it is crucial to remember that a higher EQ does not mean a creature is more likely to survive or is the fittest for life or anything of the kind—that's human hubris rearing its big head again. Fish and reptiles have been around a lot longer than the mammals with their 20-times-larger brains. Trilobites lasted hundreds of millions of years versus the six or seven million for hominids, just to name some examples. But our big heads do likely mean that our brains are particularly important for human ways of being in our environments.

It may be better to think of the extra large brain of humans as something like the extra long neck of giraffes. Though a bit freakish, each feature serves a purpose and each represents an evolutionary direction for the body that has allowed each species to thrive in particular niches. Brains helped us, necks helped them, echolocation helped bats, long trunks helped elephants, and so it goes. For hominids, especially as we began traveling, the brain may have helped make some behaviors possible that in turn helped us negotiate a wider range of environments. What may have begun as walking on two legs out into the savannahs of Africa—with neither a compass nor a butterfly's sense of direction—may have led to bigger heads.

Brain-Body-Environment

Much of the increase in brain size among hominids happens gradually over these millions of years. Yet there do appear to be two particularly rapid periods of growth. One has already been mentioned, occurring roughly 2.5 million years ago as forests were drying up and australopithecines began eating meat and making tools and paving the way for *Homo habilis* and others. Brain size increased steadily over the next 1.5 million years, doubling in fact. But then somewhere between 750 and 600 thousand years ago, that rate of increase jumps again, creating a "second brain boom."[6]

But why? Why would brains get bigger again so quickly?

A good place to look is the environment. Not only is there a strong relationship between the body and the mind, there is a strong relationship

5. Ibid., 259.
6. Calvin, *Brief History*, ch. 5.

Applies to so much else—
Cog w/ pay-off has to be worth pain of D.

between the body and where we live. Relatively rapid changes in the anatomy of a species often imply a relatively rapid change in the environmental niche, for example, some kind of change or disruption in the food supply. Otherwise there is no payoff for the change. (By the way, it is worth remembering that while these changes are relatively rapid only on the evolutionary clock, they are still slow by our standards—tens if not hundreds of thousands of years).[7]

Whether it is a bigger brain in humans or a longer neck in giraffes, such changes would be a waste of energy, more of a drain on the body, unless they create new advantages in the changing environment. For example, in people today, the brain constitutes only about 2 percent of our body weight on average—no great strain on our musculature to carry it around. However, using it is. The brain consumes about 20 percent of the body's metabolic resources.[8] A higher EQ means that a larger percentage of the caloric intake has to go to the brain. So the assumption is that larger brains, at least eventually, make themselves worth the metabolic effort, something like meat eating and tool-making did for the first brain boom.

With this perspective in mind then, is there a good candidate for such an environmental change three quarters of a million years ago? Maybe, but it is not a major ice age this time. This change would have more to do with compasses and butterflies than ice sheets and rainfall.

Every few hundred thousand years, the magnetic field surrounding our planet—sheltering us from lethal solar winds—reverses itself. It can take thousands of years to do so, but in the process, the field goes a little haywire, fracturing and tangling the magnetic axis into several norths and souths around the globe. You might see the northern lights over Hawaii and your compass would give you fits. While some believe we are due for such a change any time now, we do know the last reversal of the magnetic poles occurred 780 thousand years ago.[9]

Why would this matter? This matters to environmental niches because the magnetic field is crucial to the migration and homing behavior

---

7. Some changes and variations happen with each new generation—bigger and smaller brains, longer and shorter necks, higher and lower metabolisms, older and younger points of maturation, for example—but from an evolutionary point of view, over thousands and thousands of years, there is a general drift toward the changes that prove to be worth the price of the ticket.

8. Klein and Edgar, *Dawn*, 145.

9. For two websites providing clear and non-technical explanations of magnetic pole reversal, see Groleau, "Magnetic Field"; and NASA, "Magnetic Field."

of all kinds, if not most, creatures on earth, including monarch butterflies, fruit flies, rats, birds, whales, turtles, and even bacteria.[10] To illustrate, when researchers at the University of Kansas placed monarch butterflies in a setting where the magnetic field could be manipulated, they found that the butterflies were clearly relying upon magnetism for direction. When the field was left alone, these fall migrants headed southwest, as if going to their winter home in Mexico. When the field was reversed, they too reversed directions, heading northeast. When suppressed entirely, they flew all over the place—as lost as a boat in a Canadian fog.[11]

It appears that humans may be fairly odd in the animal world since they do not seem to possess this directional sixth sense, at least not now. And it may well be that the last of these global magnetic field flips 780 thousand years ago had no direct affect on the bodies of our ancestors. However, it could easily have affected their food sources—the fauna whose migration patterns were disrupted, the flora the fauna relied upon, and the pollination patterns of all kinds of insects and vegetation. All of this could have easily disrupted the food supply and demand of any local or regional environmental niche, thereby creating the kind of disruption that could have made relatively rapid changes in the brain feasible.[12]

No one knows for sure why it happened, but something led to this growth spurt in the brain. And the idea is that our bigger brains were allowing us do something that helped us survive the new environmental situation. Something that our predecessors were doing with their larger brains helped them to survive in the midst of (possibly) changing environments. But herein lies another puzzle. What were they doing with this newfound brainpower? Nobody knows, but it makes sense to look again for clues in the artifact record, the tools that still remain our primary texts when trying to interpret the mind of earlier hominids.

10. The October 12, 2001, issue of *Science* magazine has three helpful articles/reports on this issue: Němec et al., "Magnetoreception"; Lohmann et al., "Regional Magnetic Fields"; and Brown, "Animal Magnetism."

11 Etheredge et al., "Monarch butterflies."

12. Again, this is relatively rapid on the evolutionary clock for anatomical change, but magnetic shifts happen slowly enough that species have time to adjust. All of this is a good reminder that when it comes to addressing the issue of global warming, the problem is not simply one of changes in the environment, which, as we've seen, have been happening for millions of years. The issue is the speed of change.

Tooling Around?

After the Acheulean period, the next significant change in the style of tool-making is called the Mousterian tradition, named for the Le Moustier rock shelters of France where they were first discovered. This new style marks the beginning of what archeologists call the Middle Stone Age (in Africa).[13] Not only does this tradition include a wider variety of tools—from scrapers and blades to projectile points—they were made in a way that reveals a potential cognitive shift. These tools were made in stages.

First, like the Acheulean hand axe before, the core was shaped into a particular shape, but the difference is that this shape was not the final form, only an intermediate one, not used for anything else. Only after this intermediate form was created were the flakes knapped off from it, creating points and blades that were already sharp and shaped to the final product. It would be a little like creating a mold, except rather than putting material into the mold, material is removed. The point is that this intermediate stage would demand an even longer attention span, including what we think of now as delayed gratification.[14] With the earlier chopper and hand axe, the core was likely the primary tool, with the flakes being a (potentially useful) byproduct. With the Mousterian tradition, the flake is the final product, and the core is shaped to create the desired form of the flake.

So, the mind at work in Mousterian tool-making would certainly benefit from more brainpower. The problem is that the Mousterian tradition of tool-making does not appear on the scene until about 300 thousand years ago, several hundred thousand years after the brain boom.[15] So what were hominids doing with their newfound brainpower before the Middle Stone Age? It was not improving the hand axe. Like the Odulwan tradition before it, the Acheulean style also lasts for about a million years—up to, through, and hundreds of thousands of years past, the growth spurt three quarters of a million years ago. Bigger brains, higher EQ, same old axe.

In all it appears that our bigger-headed ancestors were not making technological improvements—not improving the hand axe, not making spears or arrows or trading beads for them, not making shelters, or doing

---

13. See McBrearty and Brooks, "Revolution," for a discussion of the complexities and challenges of the archeological designations of *Stone Age* (Africa) and *Paleolithic* (Eurasia).

14. This is called the *Levallois* method, shaping the core into a certain form first, then removing the flakes.

15. McBreaty and Brooks, "Revolution," 485ff.

anything else that leaves evidence. Maybe they were making fires, but so far there's only the one old enough to be relevant and it actually predates the brain boom. Perhaps the most striking lack of evidence is that relating to the use of bones. Later, that is, more recently, animal bones were used for all kinds of art and tools—carved into figures, scored and decorated, and crafted into needles and tools. Bones would have been plentiful, seemingly easy to work with, and would have survived time. But bone working does not even begin to show up before the Middle Stone Age.

Of course, lack of proof is not proof. But based on the fossil record for artifacts so far, if there were changes in the minds of our ancestors 750 thousand years ago to correspond with their bigger brains, the changes are invisible, as invisible as the magnetic fields directing the monarchs and protecting the earth itself from the five-billion-year-old sun.

A Good Arm

So what were the bigger brains up to? William Calvin believes one good candidate for this use of brainpower does in fact have to do with food supplies and hunting, even if the tools do not change.[16] While it was the same old axe, maybe our ancestors began using it in new ways, ways that benefited from "more mind," which itself may have benefited from "more brain." Not only is the Acheulean axe well crafted for scraping, it's aerodynamic. The axe is well suited for throwing, and as such could be used for hunting animals some distance away.

But here's the catch: even though the axe is well suited for throwing, our ancestors likely were not, at least at first. While other great apes can and do throw objects, they are not very good at it, especially compared to what even young human children now can do. "Accurate throws," Calvin, a neurologist, is quick to point out, "make a lot of demands on the brain."[17] Not only does the throw itself demand a more fine-tuned relationship in the nervous system between the brain and the nerves and muscles of the rest of the body, a good throw takes good concentration. We usually call it "focus," a kind of attention of the mind devoted to the task of getting the body ready while at the same time attending to the target of the throw. Perhaps this is an extension of the kind of focus needed to knap the Acheulean axe in the

16. See Calvin, *Brief History*, ch. 5.
17. Ibid., 47.

first place. But aiming a stone tool is a lot like aiming a boat across a foggy lake. If you are a bit off to start with, you will be way off by the end.

With practice, the focus required to knap a tool in the first place, and later to throw it, can become nearly automatic—but not at first—whether for a child or for a species. So Calvin wonders whether this growth spurt in the brain coincides with the point in our past when we shifted away from crude "side-of-the-barn throws," as he puts it (say, throwing at herds gathered at watering holes), and toward the ability to throw at particular animals, isolated, and at greater distances.[18] With herds more or less standing still and clumped together in a big mass, one could throw an axe at the crowd and take whatever is hit. But to hit a herd on the run would demand more precision as well as some timing. To hit an individual animal, say an antelope on the run, would take the skill of a baseball player, and, Calvin speculates, more brainpower—since parts of the brain devoted to other purposes would have to be called upon to help.

So even if more accurate throwing demanded more of the brain, the rewards would be tremendous—better access to food, even in times and places of leaner opportunities. The hominids who could throw like Bob Gibson (my pitching hero growing up) or my daughter Cora (a great ultimate Frisbee player), or even the family or troupe that had a great arm on its team, might do particularly well whether traveling or playing at home.[19]

∞

Though highly speculative, the idea that something like the ability to make more accurate throws could be tied to our bigger brains is intriguing. Even if wrong, it reminds us that such a skill had to evolve at some point in hominid history, especially given how poor other primates are at throwing. We went from a body and mind that could not throw very well to a body and mind that could; and a more complex brain and nervous system likely helped. It is yet another reminder of how intertwined the mind and brain and body and environment really are.

18. Ibid.

19. In Howard Gardner's theory of multiple intelligences, this would be a form of what he calls "bodily-kinesthetic intelligence," already at work in the ability to craft and use stone tools in the first place, but extended into new territory with throwing them large distances at animals on the run. If Gardner is right, each intelligence (eight total) has a deep history in our hominid past. In fact, such a deep history is one of his basic criteria for what constitutes an intelligence. See Gardner, *Frames* and *Intelligence Reframed*.

So as I watch my daughter running along the edge of a field, dipping and dodging for an opening, and as I watch her leap for the flying disc while on the run, catching it in one hand as she surveys the field for the next person to throw it to, who is also running, and then watch her actually make the throw—all this in one graceful motion—and when I think about how many millions of years it has taken to generate even the possibility of such a feat, I realize that her ability to play this sport ranks right up there with a monarch's sense of direction.

Amazing.

PART III

LISTEN CAREFULLY

In the beginning was the Word, and the Word was with God, and the Word was God. He was in the beginning with God. All things came into being through him, and without him not one thing came into being. (John 1:1–3a)

∞

AT THE END OF a beautiful day of fishing the Blackfoot River with his father and brother Paul, Norman Maclean finds his father sitting along the riverbank, reading. This is the Presbyterian minister of *A River Runs Through It*, the same who had proposed "half a billion" as a faithful compromise between religion and science.

"What have you been reading?" the son asks his father.

"A book," the minister replies, "a good book." He continues, "In the part I was reading it says the Word was in the beginning, and that's right. I used to think water was first, but if you listen carefully you will hear that the words are underneath the water."

"That's because you are a preacher first and then a fisherman," the son gently challenges. "If you ask Paul, he will tell you that the words are formed out of water."

"No," says the father, "you are not listening carefully. The water runs over the words. Paul will tell you the same thing. Where is Paul anyway?"

∞

I am forever enchanted by this little exchange between two generations of anglers, a conversation among those who are as attentive to words as they are fishing. The father is a preacher, Norman is an English professor and writer, and Paul is a journalist. Words form their lives.

The book in your hands, so far, has been exploring the origins of human knowing in relation to a much larger, older, deeper context—listening for a word below the waters of human awareness. A 14-billion-year-old universe, sea critters that thrived half a billion years ago, and a great variety of ape and hominid species, for example, help form the community of creation of which we are a part. A variety of sources and texts have been employed along the way: limestone and literature alike, our bones and the stories we tell, ancient religious words and everyday conversations.

As I see it, the challenge always, whatever the text may be, is to listen carefully, to have the ears to hear the beauty that may be revealed through them. The remarkable and, as far as we know, unique, ability of the human mind is that we can undertake this type of venture. We can use tools not only to fish for termites or chop bones, but we can use them to dig into the earth and determine dates for whatever we find. Not only can we walk on two legs or throw with amazing accuracy, we can calculate magnetic field shifts and appreciate the invisible forces at work upon bugs and brains both. Not only do we pass along genetic information from one generation to another, we pass along cultural know-how as well. We do so through watching and through words, through teaching and through learning.

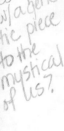

The hope running throughout the book is to gain a deeper view of life, including ourselves as knowers in it. And such a hope may too say something about human knowing, namely, that it is never quite satisfied with only seeing the surface of things. We discover meaning not only here and now in what lies before our very eyes, but tucked in behind the curtains as well, now, and as far back as we can imagine, to the beginning. And even then, we know that there is more—more to know than we could ever know.

Maybe this is a message all those texts are trying to tell us: there is more. More to life. More to ourselves. More to others than meets the eye. Maybe these are the words underneath the water.

∞

"My father went back to reading," writes Maclean, "and I tried to check what we had said by listening."[1]

1. Maclean, *River*, 103–4.

9

A Time to Talk

effect of assuming speech / robs us of mug-making / who also can speak

IN THE QUICHÉ CREATION, the Makers were not satisfied until they formed a creature that could talk—screeches and howls were not sufficient. In the beginning of Genesis, the first humans, Adam and Eve, are able to speak immediately, with each other, with God, and even with a clever serpent. The ancient Greeks as well, in telling how Prometheus and his brother Epimetheus fashioned the first mortals from the earth, never imagined humanity without words. Language is integral to our sense of life, to our sense of humanity, to knowing itself. For some, like Presbyterian preachers and anglers, religious knowing is unimaginable without the Word.

Before an evolutionary account of our origins broke open our sense of time, who could imagine human existence without speech? Why would they? But an evolutionary view, with its great reach into a deep and foggy past, forces us to consider things that don't come so naturally—for one, our ability to talk itself evolved. When? Nobody can say with certainty.

Presumably our ancestors were speaking before the ancient Sumerians began pressing wedge shapes into clay some five thousand years ago. But unlike such early writing, the spoken word leaves no trace. And it is only in the last million years that we see the kinds of anatomical changes that would make the development of spoken language—in the sense of a system of words—more feasible. Before, with a higher larynx, larger teeth, and with less motor control of the tongue, screeches and howls would have been about our speed, as they are for chimps today. If you include the bigger brain as a necessary condition, as many do, it would only be in the past few hundred thousand years, at the earliest, that we could possibly have heard a hominid word of praise to the Makers.

Even after the physical capacities are in place to create, manipulate, and differentiate a greater variety of sounds, it is still a great leap of the mind to appreciate that the combination of particular sounds (for example, the *sss* sound + *tuh* + *oh* + *nnn*) can be combined to make a new sound (*stone*), which itself stands in for something else, an object in the world. And herein rests the cognitive magic of words. They represent. Piaget called it the "semiotic function"—semiotics having to do with the study of signs and symbols. And the semiotic function represents an important developmental task of early childhood.[1] As signs, words point to something else; they are not an end in themselves. As symbols, they stand in. Words have the power to present to our minds that which is not before our eyes. As the *Popul Vuh* might say, they let us see far away.

This is to say that language requires a lot of the body and the mind. At least this is true as we think of language today, with individual words that represent objects (such as *chopper* or *tree*), or people (*you, me*), or actions (*drink, run*), or directions (*above, around*), or modifications of these (*big, fast, farther*), which can be strung together in phrases that themselves can be nested within each other or chained together in long and complex sequences that could go on infinitely, carrying ideas to another person, just as this very sentence that I am writing and that you are reading represents. Even after we have enough room in our throats and mouths to create various sounds, we need a fine-tuned nervous system to regulate breathing, the tongue, jaw muscles, lips, and more, all necessary for articulating individual words. And even with the anatomy in place, we still need a mind that can make sense of it all.

Big David

Making sense of words involves even more than understanding that individual words represent. Once we have a vocabulary of more than one or two words, we need help arranging and sorting out their meanings. Imagine that I ask the following question (better if read out loud a couple of times): *Live near of the house big David and Cora?*

The sentence is anything but clear even though none of the individual words is difficult. Perhaps the "of" is misplaced and, given that this is a question, maybe there's an implied "Do you?" Maybe I mean: Do you *live near the house* of *big David and Cora?*

1. Piaget and Inhelder, *Psychology*, ch. 3.

Better, but still a little ambiguous, is there a "little David" somewhere, a "David Junior" perhaps? Is this a nickname? Or maybe "big" modifies both David and Cora, or neither, or the house. We do this kind of thing all the time in language—fill in gaps or mentally move words around to help make sense. With more time you could probably generate several more possible meanings.

What I actually had in mind with this sentence was a word-for-word translation of the Spanish: *¿Viven circa de la casa grande David y Cora?* A clearer English translation would be: *Do David and Cora live near the big house?* In Spanish (and in many other languages) adjectives often follow the nouns they modify (*casa grande = house big*) and the word for *near* takes the preposition *of* (*circa de = near of*). Perhaps the most confusing in relation to English is that the subject often comes at the end of the sentence when asking a question, in this case two subjects, David and Cora.

A simple example, but a reminder of how much more is going on than representation alone in even a simple question. Because words can be put together in so many various ways, each language has general rules and patterns that help all who share the language sort out and structure meaning. Not only grammar and syntax, for example, but voice inflections and even pauses or silence. These patterns or rules or habits may or may not ever themselves be articulated in a society in the form of rules; they may work unconsciously. Nonetheless, such structure creates ways to help us order and interpret the individual words. When the words don't quite fit the pattern, we fill in or move words around to help.

So there are at least two major things happening with language as we know it today, two big, interrelated mind things: symbol and structure. We need to be able to understand that one thing (words, sounds) can point to or represent another, and we need to know how to arrange these signs and symbols according to some kind of system of order.[2] Both are real cognitive achievements, whether in children or the species. The combination of symbol and structure enables tremendous versatility in communication, allowing us to use the same words in different ways.

Both symbol and structure are highly social—we have to agree that this sound stands in for that, for example, *river*. We have to agree on or appreciate the rules for structuring those words: *a river runs through it* is not

---

2. I am well aware of the distinctions some scholars—mostly theologians—make between a sign and a symbol. I do not think it is a particularly helpful distinction for this conversation and is probably driven more by theology than a clear look at the how words work.

the same as *it runs through a river.* Same words, different order, different meanings. In truth, the idea that we "agree" on the sounds or rules is probably not the best word here, as it sounds like two people sitting down and hammering out a deal about the meaning of words and sentences. A better word might be "share." The parties involved must share the idea that this word means that. They have to share the general rules for putting words together. And with some important exceptions, for most human children today, this all comes seemingly naturally, much of it absorbed unconsciously before ever seeing a school.

The exceptions themselves are revealing. Children with some sort of physical challenge or brain complication, from cerebral palsy or Down's syndrome to a cleft pallet, reveal how important the physical apparatus can be. The synapses, muscles, teeth, tongue, breath, and lips all have to work well together. Autism, in its various forms, is revealing as well, since more and more it is being understood as a disruption in brain development that in turn interferes with a child's ability to share in a social world. Some would say that the inability to learn language easily is what creates the disruption in sociality in the first place, but increasingly researchers are reversing this explanation. The difficulty for the child with autism seems to be picking up the social cues and intentions of others that, in turn, make learning language much more challenging.[3]

Body, brain, and minds—language makes heavy demands upon all three. The exceptions and the rule agree. But when working well, amazing things can happen. More specifically, a potentially infinite number of combinations of words can structure thoughts and ideas in never-ending directions. One of the most powerful dimensions of language is what linguists—notably Noam Chomsky—call *recursion.*[4] Recursion is a powerful idea in itself, often used in mathematics and set theory, but in language it refers to the ways in which words and the ideas they convey can be nested within other ideas infinitely. In doing so, the very same words, phrases, clauses, sentences, and more can find new or shifting meanings when they are nested. For example, follow what happens below as words and phrases take on new meaning when nested:

3. See Simon Baron-Cohen, *Mindblindness.*

4. See Hauser et al., "Faculty of Language." The authors (including Chomsky) argue that recursion is at the heart of the uniqueness of human language, a claim that has drawn plenty of challenge and critique. Regardless, the article is a good description of recursive properties of language.

River

The Mississippi River

The Mississippi River looks gray.

She thinks the Mississippi River looks gray.

Lucy is color blind, so she thinks the Mississippi River looks gray.

The protagonist in David's novel, Lucy, is color blind, so she thinks the Mississippi River looks gray.

In the third draft, the protagonist in David's novel, Lucy, is color blind, so she thinks the Mississippi River looks gray.

In the third draft, the protagonist in David's novel, Lucy, is color blind, so she thinks the Mississippi River looks gray, but in the fourth draft he decides she can see colors.

In the third draft, the protagonist in David's novel, Lucy, is color blind, so she thinks the Mississippi River looks gray, but in the fourth draft he decides she can see colors on Sunday.

In the third draft, the protagonist in David's novel, Lucy, is color blind, so she thinks the Mississippi River looks gray, but in the fourth draft he decides she can see colors on Sunday, but then he changed his mind.

And so it goes. The possibilities are endless. The whole thing could be set within a dream or within a movie about a writer, or both. We could throw a big fat "not" at the end and change the meaning yet again. As Chomsky and his colleagues put it, "There is no longest sentence (any candidate sentence can be trumped by, for example, embedding it in 'Mary thinks that . . .')."[5] This is recursion.

Who can say, but perhaps the first whiff of the infinite that came to our ancestors—of life nested within life, of timelines within timelines, of origins within origins, of endings that never end—had something to do with the recursive word, in the beginning?

Searching for Signs

Like accurate throwing, language—with symbolic, structural, and we could add, recursive possibilities—demands so much of our bodies, brains, and

5. Ibid., 1571.

minds alike. Language, therefore, is another possible contender for contributing to and benefiting from the bigger and bigger head that begins to emerge some three quarters of a million years ago, an activity worth the price of the metabolic ticket. Language or throwing, or both.

Like accurate throwing, spoken language would leave no direct trace. Yet this fact does not stop anyone from looking for some possible indirect signs that our earlier ancestors were in fact talking to one another, other indicators of complex thought or a symbol-making minds. As the philosopher of language as well as consciousness Julian Jaynes once speculated, perhaps "each new stage of words literally created new perceptions and attentions, and such new perceptions and attentions resulted in important cultural changes which are reflected in the archaeological record."[6] Could cave paintings reflect a representational mind? Perhaps multi-staged toolmaking is a sign of more structured thought, analogous to grammar? Maybe burying the dead reflects the ability to imagine the recursive possibility of another life beyond this one? Nobody can say for sure, but language seems so key that speculation is irresistible.

Many scholars believe our species crossed a major cognitive threshold 50 thousand years ago. Though *Homo sapiens* have been around for approximately 200 thousand years, the artifact record seems to explode 50 thousand years ago. Sometimes called the "big bang of the mind" or the "dawn of human culture," or the "human revolution," the idea is that even though anatomically "modern humans" had already been around for some 150 thousand years, we crossed into new territory at this point, becoming "behaviorally modern." (The designation *Homo sapiens sapiens*, instead of just *Homo sapiens*, has sometimes been used to mark the change—the "doubly-wise human").[7]

At this point—50 thousand years ago—tools finally break from the Mousterian mold and display even more variety and complexity, in style and in substance. Wood and bone begin to supplement stone. But not only tools: necklaces and beads, sewing needles, cave paintings, carved animal figures, ritual burials, and more begin to show up on the human scene, the kinds of symbolically oriented artifacts and behaviors that we typically associate with art, religion, personal adornment, and the kind of mind that

6. Jaynes, *"Origin of Consciousness,"* 132.

7 Some—Mithen for example—suspect a "language gene" may be involved, the so-called FOXP2 gene. For an excellent discussion of the issues, and why such a genetic approach to language origins is far from simple or clear or resolved, see Michael Gazzaniga's *Human*, 33–37.

understands that one thing can stand in for another. And because words seem to work in this sort of way—spoken sounds standing in for things or places or activities[8]—many believe that language must have had something to do with this apparent explosion in creativity.

Jaynes, for one, thought so. He believed increased modifications in tool-making corresponded to linguistic modifiers (like "sharper"). Later, nouns for animals coincided with the emergence of representational cave drawings. "Once animals—particularly those that were hunted—had nouns that could designate them, they had a kind of extra being, one indeed that could be taken far back into the caves and drawn upon its walls."[9] In other words, the claim is that language created the kind of mind that generates art.

So, did the word create art?

A little extra caution on this front is important for a couple of reasons. First of all, the idea of a cognitive revolution 50 thousand years ago has important critics. Some believe it reflects more a European bias (and a romance with cave art) than the truth. Anthropologists Sally McBrearty and Alison Brooks, for example, point to many signs of "modern" behavior that can be found much earlier, in Africa, tens of thousands of years before: bone tools, evidence of fishing and long-distance trade, and the use of pigments and decoration.[10] In other words, the more that discoveries are made in Africa and the Levant, the more early signs of representational thinking and modern behavior appear. Barbed hooks of bone have been found in the Congo that are some 90 thousand years old. Beads have been found in the 70-thousand-year-old Blombos Cave site of South Africa, along with pieces of shale with interesting cross-hatched markings in them that appear intentional. Though there is some disagreement, an infant skeleton at the

---

8. Linguists call this "displacement," that is, the way words allow us to refer to things outside the context of immediate experience.

9. Julian Jaynes, "Evolution," 319.

10. Sally McBrearty and Alison S. Brooks, "Revolution," provides an excellent and highly detailed accounting of the artifact record. Through the last several decades, the cave art of Western Europe has received a lot of attention as strong evidence for the so-called big bang of the mind, a revolution starting in Europe from a group of *Homo sapiens* who evolved separately in Europe from a common ancestor a million years ago. But this so-called multi-regional theory of evolution has been fading away the last decade or two from increased evidence in Africa and the Levant for a very recent migration of Africans into Europe. See also Calvin, *Brief History*, ch. 9, for a good summary.

Border Cave site, also in South Africa, appears to have been intentionally buried, about 100 thousand years ago.[11]

It still may be the case that language played a role in the emergence of a new creativity in the species, whether 50 or 100 thousand years ago; words could have "literally created new perceptions and attentions," as Jaynes puts it. Most of us who use words for a living—writers, teachers, preachers, and the like—are eager to agree. Language generates our minds, our ability to know, the capacity to reflect upon the world, the intellect, and meaning itself. It is a kind of cognitive version of the Reverend Maclean's theology—words are beneath the waters of anything we can know.

And even for the less theologically inclined, it makes a lot of sense to us language-immersed souls who cannot imagine life, including mental life, including cultural life, apart from language. Words lead to the ability to generate representations, to make symbols, to understand that one thing can point to or stand in for another. As a result, we began to paint cave walls, carve figurines, or draw attention to ourselves with beads and paints and more. This is to say that language generates the representational mind at work in art and beauty, if not self-consciousness.

It could be.

Still, I find myself nagged by a question: Am I being a preacher first? Maybe language is less the source and more a result? It is possible that instead of the word creating art, that art created the word. Perhaps language is an extension of a mind that has already burst forth with creative possibilities. Maybe there was already something in the waters of knowing flowing through these upright-walking, tool-making, food-sharing, fire-building hominids that eventually led to a whole suite of symbol-making activities, with language being one among many. Who knows, maybe words were simply an interesting byproduct of an already beautiful mind—something like those stone flakes that are chipped off chopper cores and turn out to be good for cutting.

Then again, the preacher could have it right. Language could go back hundreds of thousands of years—stories could have been told around those earliest campfires. If this were the case, the word would indeed be even older than our species; we would not be so wrong to imagine Adam and

11 See Mithen, *Singing Neanderthals*, 251; Calvin, *Brief History*, ch. 9; and Mc-Brearty and Brooks, "Revolution," 518ff. Even the use pigments and painting may predate European usage, but this is debated. Painted slabs have been found in Namibia that could be only 26 thousand years old or could be as old as 59 thousand years old. Regarding this, see McBrearty and Brooks, "Revolution," 535–36.

Eve or the Quiché ancestors or their evolutionary equivalents 200 thousand years ago, talking, perhaps even praising their Makers or debating tempting snakes.

Or perhaps there is more, more than symbol or syntax, more than representation or structure. Whenever they came about, our recursive minds can imagine more. Such is the blessing and curse of recursion. Our ideas and theories can always be nested in more, and in fact they are, I think.

10

From Screeches to Speeches:
How Did Words Come About?

"Did you hear that?"

"I did!" Jane and I looked at our son. David was sitting in a high chair with a giant grin and dessert all over his face while we were delighting in his first words. Not "Ma-Ma" or "Pa-Pa" as we had always imagined.

"Can you believe it?"

"I know—he said *ice cream!*"

We gave him a little more.

Comparisons and Analogies

At some point, like our son, our ancestors—mine and yours—crossed a linguistic threshold. Perhaps it was only as recent as 50 thousand years ago, or it could have been 100 thousand or even a million years ago, but somebody, somewhere, said something to someone and, miraculously, someone understood. I doubt ice cream was the motivation, but I would not be surprised if food had been involved, or a *tool*, or *water*, *fire*, or a warning to *run!*

Perhaps such early language sounded something like toddler talk: *Ma-ma, Pa-pa* (which David did soon learn to say). Or, if among adults, maybe it sounded more like Tarzan talk: *Me Tarzan you Jane.* It is easy to imagine that our earliest talking ancestors, like children, started with a few words—*bear, nuts, river*—and once the vocabulary grew large enough, some kind of structuring grammar emerged to help sort out and arrange the parts into a communicable whole. It seems natural enough to compare the development of language in the species with the development of language in children today. After all, it's the closest comparison we have; a child, like the species, goes from not having language (with symbol and structure) to having it.

But there are difficulties with the comparison, difficulties born of the different contexts in which language then and now could emerge. For example, children today are immersed in a world full of words from the day they are born, if not earlier. Their minds have been swimming in language since before they can remember anything at all. By the time they go to school their heads are already a funhouse full of representational mirrors—not only words, but pictures and signs, figurines and photos, dolls and decals and more. One reading through *Goodnight Moon* or *Green Eggs and Ham*, or one episode of *Sesame Street* or any cartoon, is chock full of more representational stuff and structured sentences than Lucy could have ever imagined.

To top matters off, adults often intentionally teach babies individual words by showing them what we are talking about—*toes, apple, book*—and in this way the child can see the object or person while hearing the word, and connect the two like Pavlov's dog. (In fact this is how I taught my own dog *Frisbee*.) I think such learning, whether in a dog or in a child, is something of a minor miracle all by itself, but the point is that the first hominid word-speakers had no such teachers. No books, television, or instructors, not even conversations to overhear.

Yet, somebody somewhere said something to someone and someone understood.

From Communication to Proto-Language

The benefits of language are self-evident. For example, the ability to tell another where to find water or how to build a fire certainly seems worth the brainpower it takes. Still, as Julian Jaynes cautions, maybe we shouldn't be so sure. Even if a nonhuman primate could be taught speech or sign language and returned to the wild, "it is not at all certain that it would have the slightest survival value whatever." Why? First of all, spoken language could disrupt the signaling systems already in place and that organize social patterns. Second of all, the sounds themselves could be dangerous and attract predators. Frankly the better the species has adapted to a specific environmental niche, the more disastrous the consequences would be.[1]

Given such a caution, it is likely that language—with symbol and structure—evolved relatively gradually, possibly provoked by changes in environmental niches (ice ages or magnetic pole shifts) or by the challenges of new locations as our ancestors began traveling into new territories. Even so, compared to children now, language development would have been slow, even taking thousands of generations. This is why linguists propose some sort of *pre-language* or *proto-language* as a forerunner to full-blown representational, structured language, something in between the screech and the speech, something growing out of the kinds of communication patterns we can still see in other animals.

The fact is that since we modern humans rely so heavily upon *language* to *communicate*, we tend to use the terms synonymously. A howling monkey, a growling dog, or a screeching bird is certainly communicating in some sense, signaling to another creature to "Get away!" for example. Animals of all kinds communicate through gestures and body positions, through songs and smells, or through looks and glances. Such communication can be complex, fascinating, useful, and even beautiful to our ears—it certainly means something among its users—but the difficult question is whether or not it is of the same order as human language with its individual words arranged by a socially shared grammar.

According to most language scholars, one of the major differences between human language and that of other creatures involves time. Most animal communication seems to be concerned with the moment—now—and usually involves the attempt to make something happen very soon. When our domesticated cat meows at the door, he is trying to get me to open it right then and there so he can go through and eat his food on the other side. Nothing in his behavior leads me to believe that he is thinking that he may want to go through the door later in the day or that an open door would improve the air circulation of our home and make him more comfortable. Seeing the bigger picture, either in time or space, does not seem to be our cat's gift. He meows, I open the door, he runs through, he eats.

Linguists call this *manipulative communication*.[2] It is not manipulative in the everyday sense of the word—being scheming or underhanded—instead it is manipulative because its purpose is to bring about an immedi-

crying &
tears
fall under
this category

1. Jaynes, "Evolution," 312.
2. See Mithen, *Singing Neanderthals*, 21ff.

ate behavioral response in others. *Get back, run, keep doing that, feed me, leave me alone, submit, find me, stop, help,* or *mate with me,* to name a few examples. Even expressing this kind of communication in human words and phrases may skew our understanding too much toward human language and the kind of thoughts accompanying our words. Perhaps a better comparison would be to think about human screams or cries, forms of communication that are also concerned with the moment and making something happen immediately. A hungry baby cries and this helps bring about a feeding. Someone falls down and lets out a yell that potentially draws some help. The point is that neither cries nor yells need to employ the use of individual, differentiated words in order to make something happen.

Words as Old

It could be that the case that *Homo erectus* had a proto-language, that is, a handful of words—say, *food* or *go*—as a part of a much richer set of gestures, postures, expressions, and screeches for example. Perhaps they had a few simple, but useful, nouns or simple commands—after all, even my dog can recognize *Frisbee* and *sit*—and a handful of other words learned through basic association. Used sparingly, or for very specific purposes, there would not even be much need for grammar; context and gesturing could provide the structure. Pointing to a bush and saying *food* could go a long way, clarifying for example that what I am pointing to is not a tiger, or water, or rain on the horizon, but a berry bush. Such proto-language could be just helpful enough without totally disrupting the communication mechanisms already in place. Thousands of generation could come and go with a handful of words, and find them helpful.

Yet once a larger vocabulary builds, as the last chapter discusses, it does not take long for even a handful of simple words to become confusing or ambiguous when put together. Consider even a simple three-word phrase such as *bear-me-run*. It could mean "I saw a bear and I ran away" or "A bear saw me and it ran" or "I run like a bear" or "I ran after a bear" or "A bear is coming; I ran to warn you." The more that individual words bear the weight for communication—including contextual information—the more grammar is needed. What once was provided by sight, sound, gesture, and overall awareness of a situation we now ask grammar to supply. It is a lot to ask of our brains, so where did grammar come from?

One line of thought is that when matters got more complicated for our proto-linguistic ancestors, the mind/body/brain then drew upon other behaviors that required structure in order to help. For example, as our ancestors began to make tools in stages (involving two or three steps) or when they began to do anything that involved even the simplest of sequences, they were learning the rudiments of "structured stuff," as William Calvin puts it. The idea, as Calvin describes it, is that the seeds of grammar may have arisen independently from the seeds of word making—a kind of proto-structure. Stages at work in tool-making, in food preparation, or with axe throwing, for example, could have been generating a more and more complex nervous system that would eventually allow our ancestors to structure words in clearer ways and in more combinations, allowing us to sort out "who did what to whom."[3] Put those early words (that symbolize) together with staged thought (that structures) and you get language.

In this view proto-language consists of representational words before grammar. Words, in this case, could be very old. Nested within even older systems of manipulative communication, our ancestors a million years ago could have had a handful of words, like toddlers today, or like some of the apes who have been tutored in captivity. Grammar could come later.

Words as Young

There is another line of thought however, attractive in light of the screeches and babbles and the ways in which manipulative communication seems to work. In this alternative view of proto-language, words come very late in the game. In this view proto-language can be thought of as a new set of cries or phrases but without individual words.

Julian Jaynes, for example, was an early proponent of this view, suggesting the possibility that the roots of human language rest in an "incidental call system" of cries and yells that would accompany visual gestures of warning or summons. In this scenario, the visual signaling was the primary means of communication—the facial expressions, postures, and movements that communicated a message immediately. Sounds were secondary, "incidental," simply adding emotional intensity to bodily communication, helping to draw attention to the visual signals in the first place. So, based upon comparisons with other primate calling systems, Jaynes suggests that hominids 400 thousand years ago may have had a call system composed of

3. Calvin, *Brief History*, 85.

15 to 20 cries—manipulative, immediate, and similar to other apes. But, as the brain continued to grow, and as complex behaviors increasingly occupied the hands, those cries may have begun to move out of the incidental background and into the more intentional foreground. Jaynes dubs it the "encephalization of vocalization," the growth of vocalization; screeches began to matter and could communicate more directly.[4] In this view, meaningful, intentional cries and howls precede any particular word.

But wouldn't such cries be the equivalent of words?

Not quite. Language scholar Alison Wray, more recently, helps us understand the difference. Her approach to proto-language also involves words coming along late in the game. For her, proto-language involves not discrete words, but discrete utterances. These utterances (or messages, or chunks, or phrases, or formulae—many terms abound in the literature) are not only manipulative and intentional; they are holistic. Unlike a sentence, if taken apart, the utterance would not yield individual words. As she put it, "there are no component parts that could be recombined to create a new message."[5]

For example, as a rough analogy she offers the magical phrase *abracadabra*. It could mean "I am doing magic now" or "Watch and see the rabbit disappear" or "Handkerchiefs are going to turn into doves" or "I am saying something magical because that's what magicians do" or "Look here because something strange will happen." Wray calls it a "structurally noncompositional sequence" that means something like "I hereby cast a spell on this object/person, causing a desirable change."[6] Even though we all know what the phrase means, it takes so many words to explain or translate, with no perfect fit. More to the point, you cannot break the phrase apart and use the pieces like words. If *a-bra-ca-da-bra* means "I am now casting a spell" it does not follow that *ba-bra-ca-da-bra* means "You are now casting a spell." Or, *sha-bra-ca-da-bra* does not mean "The tiger is about to cast a spell." Unlike sentences with words, these holistic phrases don't use interchangeable parts like that. And in fact, the phrases are irreducible to translations that use words.

In this approach to proto-language words could be relatively young. And without individual words there is no need for grammar.

---

4. Jaynes, "Evolution," 316.
5. Wray, "Protolanguage," 51.
6. Wray and Grace, "Consequences," 27.

An added benefit to whole phrases is that they are easier to remember. In the same way that chunking a phone number or series of numbers is easier to remember than the individual numbers, so it is with phrases generally.[7] For example, the series *one-four-nine-two-one-nine-five-eight* is much harder to remember if memorized as a series of individual numbers. It is perhaps easier if spoken in the form of a phone number: 149-2195, extension 8. It is much easier if chunked into two dates: 1492 and 1958. Whole phrases may not have been very flexible, but they may have been easier to remember, and good enough to do a lot. And with a larger and more complex brain, perhaps a greater and greater repertoire of holistic phrases could have been remembered and utilized.

A comparison to babies may be appropriate in this case. Before words, as most every parent or caretaker soon learns, there are different kinds of cries, and over time one learns to sense the patterns in them. Some cries are hungry, some mad, some express the need for changing or some other discomfort, and so it goes. It is manipulative communication still rooted in the moment, trying to make something happen. While it is not a perfect system—sometimes we parents never figure it out—still, a lot can be communicated in a cry, nearly from the first breath. So it is not hard to imagine, in a way not so different from parents, that the bigger-brained hominids 750 to 500 thousand years ago, more and more, began to pay attention to such patterns in one another's cries, screeches, and howls.

In this approach to proto-language, phrases could be very old, but words relatively young.

Emotional Intensity

Even with a younger view of words, and a holistic view of proto-language, at some point somebody somewhere said something—in the form of a word—to someone and someone understood. Somehow discrete phrases differentiated into words that eventually could be recombined with other words to create a potentially infinite number of new phrases. But how?

In our age of computers and artificial intelligence, it may be a little too easy to think of language along the lines of information processing. Words *compute* or not, specific languages are like *software* for our *hardwired* brains, communication is reducible to *bits* of information in a series of ones and zeros. Like all analogies or metaphors, these are interesting

7. Wray, "Protolanguage," makes this point.

comparisons, with truth to be found in them. But there are differences. To think of language as information processing, to think of intelligence as a kind of mathematical logic, to think of knowing itself along the lines of a computer program misses so much, especially what makes meaning feel meaningful. Symbols, syntax, and even recursion do not come to life without some emotional help. What computer processing metaphors miss when it comes to language is feeling. And it is possible that emotional intensity gave rise to individual words in the first place.

Manipulative communication in our fellow mammals makes things happen by evoking responses in others. Signals can be low-key and relaxed (*hello*), or fraught with fear or aggression (*back off now!*). The responses evoked can range in the same way (*hello to you too* or *you back off!*). The ability to understand, at this level of communication, is basic, behavioral, meaningful, rich with desires and fears, and much older than individual words in anyone's theory of language. All kinds of affective signaling may be involved—from postures and glares to facial expressions and breathing patterns. Importantly, these signs of our emotional lives do not go away just because we have developed language.

In Jaynes's theory of language origins, emotional intensity plays a key role in the development of words. For example, earlier hominids may have had a warning cry for an approaching predator, such as *wah! wah! wah!* It didn't matter whether it was a bear or a tiger. But if the danger became extremely close, the cry might have intensified, sounding more like *wahee!* Being really scared easily changes the sound of a voice. If the threat is far away, perhaps the cry is more relaxed, a *wahoo!*[8] The important point here is that emotion can vary the sound of the cries—as it does for babies, dogs, apes, and for you and me. By doing so, these variations over time began to communicate something even more specific than fear or warning. Through time, repetition, and imitation, a *wahee* could have come to mean that a threat is close, for example (and still not matter whether the threat is a bear or tiger), and a *wahoo* could have come to mean that a threat is far away. In this scenario, the qualifiers actually "precede the invention of the nouns that they modified." The first words in this case were not nouns such as *food* or *tool* or *ice cream* or *run*; the first words were these endings, the modifiers, the equivalent to *near* and *far*.[9]

8. Jaynes , "Evolution," 317.

9. Ibid. Jaynes's dating of language origins plays off of the artifact record—too specifically and speculatively in my view. For example, modifiers come 40–50 thousand years

In addition, emotional intensity may have helped raise the importance of the sounds themselves, moving them out of the background of communication and into the foreground; then such intensity could have helped raise the importance of sounds within sounds, differentiations that contained clues about what to do (like *run* or *not*).[10] In other words, our ancestors had good reason to listen even more carefully to one another. The ones who learned to listen may have avoided becoming dinner for a tiger.

As important as not being eaten would be, there may have been even more going on. As Stanley Greenspan and Stuart Shanker suggest, more and more—nested in the rich and increasingly complex emotional signaling of our ancestors—the sounds themselves may have brought pleasure. This would be the birth of talk for talk's sake. Greenspan and Shanker point to the ways in which toddlers discover "that vocalizations and/or words can be as much a source of closeness and shared pleasure as a warm hug." As they describe it, "The baby moves from hugs and caresses to shared vocalizations and communication through emotional signaling as a way of satisfying this fundamental need for nurturance. It is remarkable how, as adults, humans can feel the same nurturing warmth over the telephone with people thousands of miles away simply by hearing the warmth in their voices and basking in the meaning of their words."[11] In other words, just as babies and toddlers find pleasure, comfort, and closeness in vocalizing, so it may have been for our ancestors, before, during, and after the development of words.

In this view, words could be old or young, but they reflect rich emotional lives.

∞

The screeches and howls of chimps and dogs and babies remind us of the emotional power of communication resting beneath grammar and symbol, beneath the recursive possibilities of human language.[12] And our words still have the potential to evoke feelings and behaviors in others, imme-

---

ago, corresponding to increased modifications in tools; animal nouns come some 25–30 thousand years ago, with the appearance of cave drawings. Personal names for humans come later, as recently as 10–12 thousand years ago, with the rise of agriculture.

10. Ibid., and Jaynes, "Consciousness," 129ff.

11. Greenspan and Shanker, *First Idea*, 206.

12. For more on this point, see Tomasello, *Human Communication*, ch. 2.

diately, and over time. Meaning, in other words, involves more than the computational logic of word order or the ability to represent or symbolize. And without this *more*—this powerful set of social interactions intertwined with the affective life—meaning, in the end, would not be very meaningful.

What's in a Name

In general, there is little evidence that animals other than humans use language in anything but manipulative, immediate ways; and the assumption is that hominids first communicated likewise. My dog, living in a domesticated human world, may be able to connect a few words like *Frisbee* or *sit* to objects or behaviors through simple association, but even these seem locked in the immediacy of stimulus and response. If I say "Get the Frisbee" she finds the disc and runs to the door with it. If I say "Hide the Frisbee" or "Throw the Frisbee to me" or just plain "Frisbee" she still finds the disc and runs to the front door with it. Human words are very basic to her. I'm sure she receives much more interesting and complex messages from her sense of smell.

Even so, there are some cases where chimps and bonobos (our two closest primate relatives) seem not only able to associate words with objects and actions, but are able to generate words through sign language or so-called lexigram boards (keyboards with symbols instead of letters). These examples are intriguing, but of course not what happens in the wild.[13] The closest thing to the natural use of something like the human use of words may be among bottlenose dolphins, who, according to the research of Vincent Janik of Scotland's St. Andrews University, seem to be using specific whistles to indicate specific dolphins. In other words, these dolphins may be naming each other.[14]

On the one hand, these dolphins should give us pause, offering yet another reminder of how our notions of language are deeply locked into human ways of thinking or hearing or producing sounds. On the other hand, the notion that specific whistles may be working among dolphins the way humans use proper nouns—to name—raises another possibility. It

---

13. Greenspan and Shanker, *First Idea*, has an extensive discussion of such studies, especially ones with Kanzi, a bonobo with an impressive vocabulary on the lexigram board.

14. Janik et al., "Signature Whistle."

could be that we didn't just screech our way into the linguistic universe, but whistled, hummed, or drummed our way into it.

There is the possibility that some form of music rests beneath our words, if not our screeches. Or the screeches themselves may have been more musical than anyone has realized.

At some point, somebody, somewhere, *sang* something to someone and someone understood.

11

Rhythm of the Saints

EARLIER THIS WEEK, HOLY Week, someone put out a call for drums: *Any who have them bring your percussion instruments to church, bring extras if you can—we are going to have an Easter drum circle.*

Today is Easter and, sure enough, the hand drums have come—congas, bongos, djembes, talking drums, doumbeks, and more—representing cultures from around the world. But not only drums, someone has brought a whole basket full of egg-shaped shakers, enough that every child can have one. There are guiros and tambourines, wooden blocks and claves, cowbells and a triangle. It is a percussionist's dream.

As the congregation, full of Easter spirit, is flowing out the front doors of the church and onto the round plaza, itself shaped like a drum head, people are being greeted with the crazy yet coordinated sounds of life. And any who want, but especially the children, are encouraged to grab a drum or shaker and jump into these resurrection rhythms. They are. And those who are not are dancing or clapping are walking with a little more spring and smile. Strolling by the drum I am playing, an octogenarian slaps the skin, "makes you feel alive," he says.

I'm still smiling.

Our Musical Ancestors

Charles Darwin, in his *Descent of Man*, suspects that music predates speech in the origins of the species. Language, for Darwin, is a more recent development, one built on top of a wilder, sexier foundation. Our "progenitors," Darwin theorizes, "either males or the females, or both sexes, before they had acquired the power of expressing their mutual love in articulate language, endeavored to charm each other with musical notes and rhythm."[1]

The idea is one that many scholars have continued to support over the century and a half since Darwin proposed it. The aesthetic appeal of music would have corresponded to the aesthetic appeal of a potential mate. Beautiful music, beautiful people. Music attracts and connects. Along the way, music would also be a form of emotional expression. Beautiful feelings—attraction, attachment, desire, gratitude, well-being, satisfaction—give rise to beautiful sounds and rhythms that reinforce those feelings. Love makes music and music makes love.

For Darwin, speech and music today continue to reflect their deeper roots. "The impassioned orator, bard, or musician, when with his various tones and cadences he excites the strongest emotions in his hearers," writes Darwin, "little suspects that he uses the same means by which, at an extremely remote period, his half-human ancestors aroused each other's ardent passions during their mutual courtship and rivalry."[2]

But there is another direction of thinking about the origins of music. Rather than courtship, this school of thought looks to parenting, that is, to the role of musical interactions between parent (often assumed to be mothers, but that may be a flawed assumption) and child. While Sigmund Freud would consider both kinds of loving interactions as ultimately cut from the same libidinous fabric, the emphasis here is not upon attracting or keeping a mate but upon keeping the kids happy. The more our ancestors began to use their arms and hands for everyday purposes such as picking berries, knapping tools, or throwing axes, for example, the greater the dilemma would have been concerning what to do with the baby.

Most mammals require some sort of intense care early on in their lives—feeding, protection from predators, help or patience with mobility. The longer the period of a child's development occurs *outside* the womb, the longer is this period of dependence upon caregivers. The bigger and bigger heads of our hominid ancestors led to even longer and longer periods of development outside the womb for those brains to mature. But this requires longer and longer periods during which parental arms and attention are tied up with the child. In other words, without a handy kangaroo pouch human caregivers may have sought ways to keep baby safe and still be able

1. Darwin, *Descent*, 585.
2. Ibid., 586.

to use their arms. Cooing, humming, or other soothing sounds could have been the first babysitter.

Steven Mithen calls it the "putting down baby" theory. Setting the baby down, nearby, for short periods would free up the mother for other important activities. But to keep the baby happy, she could still use "eye contact, gestures, expressions and utterances to reassure the infant, these being substitutes for the physical contact that the infant would desire."[3] In these "utterances" the theory goes, were the first human melodies. Like eye contact, like smiles, prelinguistic communication through a melodic and/ or rhythmic voice represents a "mother and child reunion," as Simon and Garfunkel once sang, extending the connection between the two through space with sound.

In either case, whether music emerged as an ally to the love between adults, or as a bridge to parental care between the generations, or both, we can notice at least two dimensions of music common to both directions of thought. One is that music is highly social, drawing and holding people together. Another is that music is deeply tied to human emotions, able to generate or express intense feeling that words do not fully capture. We know this is true for humans today; whether singing a lullaby to a newborn or gathering in a drum circle, whether joining in a congregational hymn or dancing at a prom, music gathers and holds communities of people together, often with powerful emotional intensity known through tears of delight and sadness alike. *Recog. music / ability sing when lang lost = evidence*

The possibility that human music is older than human speech is a strong one. To many of us, it *feels* older. Though not a scientifically based conclusion, nonetheless, music feels as if it flows from and touches some deep part of ourselves. It may be no accident that music is so tangled up with the sacred in human knowing. Most religious gatherings in the world today rely upon music in some form—drums and organs, singing and chanting, dirges and processionals, even rhythmic breathing—to help mark off the times and places touched by the sacred. Running beneath the river of our theological minds and religious doctrines, underneath words even, may be the rhythms and melodies of our ancient ancestors, connecting us to life. *precur. so to speech?*

3. Mithen, *Singing Neanderthals*, 201.

Hmmmm-ing Along

Not only Darwin, but many in his wake, have proposed that music lies underneath language, that melody and rhythm were used by the human voice before words and grammar. And this may well be true. But the reverse is possible as well: that music was an offshoot or side effect of language. As our ancestors were chattering away, warning of lions and tigers and bears, or telling one another where a good blueberry bush could be found, someone discovered the musical qualities in those voiced words and began to isolate them. It is possible that words came before music, but I am doubtful. Then again, perhaps there is no need to choose.

In his book *The Singing Neanderthals*, Steven Mithen proposes a theory of language origins that not only represents a form of proto-language but one that is simultaneously a form of proto-music. Mithen believes that both music and language arose from a single precursor. "Hmmmm" he playfully calls it, an acronym for *h*olistic, *m*anipulative, *m*ulti-*m*odal, and *m*usical. The theory is that music and language flow from a common source, a "musilanguage"[4] that later, in *Homo sapiens* alone, branched off into two different directions—music and language.

It is similar to the approaches of Julian Jaynes and Allison Wray in that the Hmmmm of our ancestors was *holistic*; whole messages only later differentiate into more discrete word components. It was *manipulative*, as discussed in the last chapter, in that it functioned to make something happen immediately—attracting a mate for example, or soothing a child's distress. In addition, manipulative communication not only evokes behaviors but can evoke emotional states as well. It can create feelings in another. On top of the holistic and manipulative aspects of this early communication, it was *multi-modal* in that bodily gestures, dancing, and facial expressions, for example, accompanied sounds.

While all these dimensions of communication have been pointed out before in theories of language origins, Mithen has done so with a fascinating twist, pointing to another quality of the audible communication of so much of the animal world: it is *musical*. The musical quality may be most obvious in the songs of birds with their changing pitches and melodies, but a wolf's howl, a cricket's rhythmic chirping, a rooster's crow, or perhaps even a baby's babbling, for example, also involve dynamics such as pitch

---

4. Ibid., 26. Mithen borrows the term from Brown, "Musilanguage."

changes and glides, repetition and harmonization, in short, melody and rhythm.

Mithen's general survey of primate, especially great ape, communication, leads him to conclude that most primate communication shares in all these features of Hmmmm, often serving a social function among them. For example, he points to the work of Bruce Richman, who spent eight years studying the Gelada monkeys of the Ethiopian highlands.[5] Richman found that the monkeys are constantly chattering. "As they approach one another, walk past one another or take leave of one another, as they start or stop social grooming, as they threaten someone because he is too close to a partner, solicit someone's support or reassurance, in fact, as they do the infinite variety of different social actions that make up the minute-to-minute substance of their social lives they always accompany these actions with vocalizing." Through all these varieties of social interactions these vocalizations themselves employ a rich use of rhythm and melody: "Fast rhythms, slow rhythms, staccato rhythms, glissando rhythms; first-beat accented rhythms, end-accented rhythms; melodies that have evenly spaced musical intervals covering a range of two or three octaves; melodies that repeat exactly, previously produced, rising or falling musical intervals; and on and on."[6]

The Gelada present a wonderful example of how musical some primate communication can be. This is the case even as other primate communication may not be so musical, relying more upon gestures or bodily positions for example. The physiology of the species and the ecological history and niches will have a lot to say about the nature and necessity of the communication patterns employed. But the point is, in Mithen's words, "The holistic, manipulative, multi-modal, and musical characteristics of ape communications systems provide the ingredients for that of the earliest human ancestors, living in Africa six million years ago, from which human language and music ultimately evolved."[7]

So, in these cues from other primates, may be clues to early hominid communication—a musical, gestural, emotional, manipulative form of proto-music-language that served the social life, not to mention the survival, of the species. And by recognizing our connection to our primate

5. For a short video of the monkeys, see *National Geographic*, "Gelada Monkeys."

6. Richmond, "Rhythm and Melody," 199, quoted in Mithen, *Singing Neanderthals*, 110.

7. Mithen, *Singing Neanderthals*, 121.

cousins, it is easier to notice how multilayered and complex all those so-called screeches and howls may have actually been and how much such complexity may still rest beneath human language and human music today.

As Mithen listens carefully to the sounds and rhythms of our languages today, he, like Darwin, hears something musical underneath the waters. When a child learns to say her ABCs to the tune of "Twinkle Twinkle Little Star," or when I still hear that song in my head when I am alphabetizing or filing, we are somehow closer to our musical-linguistic roots. That is, words and music share a common trunk. In time, language—as we know it today—branched one way; music—which, like language, has become as thoroughly complex and structured as well—branched another. This is to say that Bach canons and poly-rhythmic drum circles reveal that music too has taken a long strange trip of its own.

One More M

Mithen suggests adding one more *m* to this early musical language—*mimesis*—making it Hmmmmm. All the other *m*'s (as well as the *h*), are drawn from contemporary comparisons to other animals. Mimesis, however, is drawn from evidence of a firmer sort—those stone tools that could go hundreds of thousands of years with few signs of change or innovation. What if tool-making had not been the only manner of imitation occurring among our ancient ancestors? What if they began imitating sounds, whether those produced by their fellows or those produced by the animal world around them? What would this add to the communicative abilities of, say *Homo erectus*, a million years ago? It could be that mimesis—the ability to mimic, imitate, mime, or some variation of any or all of these—brought about new possibilities in communication.

As Mithen speculates, what if holistic phrases were accompanied by mimesis? As an example, perhaps there was a holistic phrase for "share food with" that was then "followed by a pointing gesture towards an individual or mimesis of that individual."[8] Or imagine that *ahh-ooo-gah* is a holistic phrase with the equivalent meaning of "hunt animal with me." Then imagine that accompanying the phrase was a mimesis of the particular animal, say the growl of a bear or the waddle of a duck. This would be "a highly evolved form of 'Hmmmmm' communication" compared to that of earlier hominids and other primate species. It could also be the case that such

8. Ibid., 172.

communication was challenging enough to begin demanding more of the brain but also provide enough benefit to be worth the price of the ticket. Such communication would still have been limited enough to square with the fact that there are few signs in the artifact record of much creativity or innovation until the most recent few hundred thousand years.

Essentially Mithen's position is that the varieties of the Homo species, going back nearly two million years and including the Neanderthals as recently as 30 thousand years ago, used a form of Hmmmmm communication, but not language as we know it today. Over time and with larger brains these communications may have become more varied (than a handful of calls and cries) and frequent, becoming increasingly important to the social cohesion and daily functioning of these hominids. But segmentation into language with representational words and grammatical structure would only come into being with *Homo sapiens* in the last 200 thousand years, slowly at first, but crossing a threshold 50 thousand years ago, when we see so many signs of a symbol-generating mind. (In light of the discussion in last chapter, and earlier signs of representational thought, we could back the date up to 100 thousand years ago without much trouble to the theory.[9]) At this point, music and language take their own paths.

The Direct Power of Music

So it could be the case, as Darwin proposed, that music is simply older than language. Or it could be that music and language were completely intertwined for hundreds of thousands of years in the kind of scenario Mithen describes. In either case, music is deeply tied to the emotional life of the species, connecting us to one another in deep and powerful ways, as well as connecting us to our own feelings. Of course words can evoke the passions as well, but tend to do so indirectly, by representing ideas that move us, or offend. For the sheer sounds of words to move us—something a poet or rapper does intentionally—the sounds draw from the musical qualities of speech, using pitch and rhythm, modulations of duration and intensity. As Darwin pointed out, the best public speakers—from politicians and preachers to storytellers and actors—know how to bring words to musical life through sound, if not accompanied by a few good gestures as well.

9. Mithen recognizes the debates, and particularly the challenge offered by McBreaty and Brooks (see previous chapter), but still believes, at the least, in a "demographic and cultural threshold" occurring about 50 thousand years ago. Ibid., 262.

But music is a bit different, more direct. All by themselves, rhythms and melodies have the power to enchant or disturb us, if not make our feet move—all without a word. By "direct" I mean that music can affect us immediately like a wonderful view from a mountain, or a repulsive odor, or a cool breeze on a hot day. We may feel joy or wonder, agitation or relief from the sounds and rhythms themselves. The directness of music reminds us that there is a layer of experiencing the world around us, even in us, that is not dependent upon language and interpretation and representation to be known. With language, we need to know how to interpret the words being used, what they represent. Trying to read an unknown language in print may best illustrate the point. We cannot pick up any of the musical qualities of the language when experienced only visually.

Of course, over time, as with everything else in human culture, we do interpret music, compare one piece to old ones, accumulate memories and experiences with particular melodies, and reminisce over the feelings evoked by a song played at a prom or a hymn sung at church. Like language, music can be used to represent something else—ideas, emotions, common experiences. This is often the function of a musical score in film: to evoke emotions and moods in order to intensify the scene. Consider the ominous bass notes of an invisible underwater threat in *Jaws*, or the high-pitched strings of the terrifying shower scene in *Psycho*, or the romantic sweeping symphonies of the *Star Wars* films. Musical compositions can function like words—representing something else—but the larger point is that they draw their initial power from an experience that is more direct than words.

Clicking with the Dead

Oliver Sacks, the neurologist and popular author of such works as *Awakenings, The Man Who Mistook His Wife for a Hat,* and *An Anthropologist on Mars*, relays a powerful musical experience he shared with one of his patients, an experience that helps illustrate the special role of music in the human soul. In his book *Musicophilia* Sacks describes Greg F., who had a tumor that destroyed his memory and most of his spontaneity—"he had been amnesic and inert, barely responsive except to music for many years." Sacks took Greg to a Grateful Dead concert held at Madison Square Garden. "The music, the rhythm, got everyone within seconds. I saw the whole vast arena in motion with the music, eighteen thousand people dancing, transported, every nervous system there synchronized to the music." Not only did Sacks the scientist shed his "usual diffidence and inhibition," getting all caught up in the crowd of dancing, so did Greg. He "was taken over and animated by the thumping, pounding excitement of the crowd around him, the rhythmic clapping and chanting, and soon he, too, began shouting the name of one of his favorite songs, 'Tobacco Road, Tobacco Road!'"[10]

Sacks, goes on to discuss the power of music—rhythm in particular—to bring people together, whether through sacred worship, military marching, or a jam band. Rhythm binds communities through sound and movement, sometimes to the ecstasy of religious feeling, martial excitation, or musical joy. Rhythm is powerful, able to "move people," as Sacks puts it, "in both senses of the word," and may have played an important role in human evolution by "producing a sense of collectivity and community."[11] As a drummer myself, in nightclubs with a band as well as in sanctuaries with congregational singing, I can only give an amen to Sacks' point; there is something deeply compelling and deeply binding about the repetition of patterns of sound, what I have come to think of as the *mimesis of sound.*

At its heart, rhythm is repetition, an imitation of sound. "Strike a membrane with a stick," writes Mickey Hart, drummer for the Grateful Dead, "the ear fills with noise—unmelodious, inharmonic sound. Strike it a second time, a third, you've got rhythm." Hart's origin story goes like this: "In the beginning was noise. And noise begat rhythm. And rhythm begat everything else. This is the kind of cosmology a drummer can live with."[12]

The transformation that takes place between noise and rhythm is a type of recursion, one between sound and silence and sound again, in potentially infinite repetitions and combinations. On the one hand, each beat is unique in that it takes place at a particular place in time, but then again, each successive beat is an imitation in time of the one before, set off by the silence in between. Each beat is given its individual moment in time. Each beat is a repetition, part of a collective that when taken all together creates a pattern in the airwaves known directly through our listening bodies.

In the end it may be no accident that the awareness of *the beginning*—of time itself—may be tied to rhythm, to the mimesis of sound, to repetition. Rhythm is about keeping time.

Perhaps beneath language as we know it—behind the melodies and harmonies as we hear them today—is a steady backbeat of sound drawing

10. Sacks, *Musicophilia*, 245.
11. Ibid., 246.
12. Hart, *Drumming*, 12.

listeners together into a communal form of knowing, a shared
hat synchronizes the hearts if not the dancing feet of our ances-
ourse I am thinking like a drummer, but sometimes I can almost
hear the steady *click, click, click* of stone striking stone to create a beautiful
hand axe and a powerful rhythm. It would get my attention. But whether
the noise of each strike transformed into a rhythm in the ears of our tool-
making ancestors one million years ago, or even two million, is anyone's
guess.

The Ties That Bind

Language, music, structure, recursion, mimesis, knowing—how key is
rhythm? How key is rhythm to the mind of the species? My own answer
cannot be extricated from years of conga beats, claves, and a certain congregation full of life. But consider the final words from Oliver Sacks in his
essay on rhythm as he discusses, from a neuroscientific point of view, the
"binding problem" in perception. The problem is: What holds perception
together? "What enables us, for example, to bind together the sight, sound,
smell, and emotions aroused by the sight of a jaguar? Such binding in the
nervous system is accomplished by rapid, synchronized firing of nerve cells
in different parts of the brain. Just as rapid neuronal oscillations bind together different functional parts within the brain and nervous system, so
rhythm binds together the individual systems of a human community."[13]

Given that Gelada monkeys use it in their communication, it is quite
possible that rhythm is older than hominids themselves, from seven million
years ago and before, binding one to another like the breath of the Creator
in Genesis, breathing life into the dust of the earth. Or was it a song? In the
words of one theologian: "In the quickening breath and through the form-
giving word, the Creator sings out his creatures in the sounds and rhythms
in which he has his joy and his good pleasure." Jürgen Moltmann calls this
the *song of creation*, and if we listen carefully we can hear in the song the
"the innermost life of the world."[14] And the music is very good.

13. Sacks, *Musicophilia*, 247.
14. Moltmann, *Way of Jesus Christ*, 289.

PART IV

THE BUTTERFLY EFFECT

MANY YEARS AGO THE scientist Edward Lorenz posed a strange question: "Does the flap of a butterfly's wings in Brazil set off a tornado in Texas?"[1] In 1961, at MIT, Lorenz was working with an early computer to simulate and graph out weather patterns. With the rapid calculating abilities of these new machines, numbers could now be used to represent certain weather conditions and calculate changes in them. One day Lorenz wanted to reproduce a graph he had generated before. But this time he took a shortcut—a tiny, seemingly insignificant shortcut with the numbers—he used the fraction 0.506 instead of 0.506127. It was tiniest fraction of the fraction.

When the graph began printing it looked identical to the previous one. The shortcut made no visible difference as the infinitesimal change was far narrower than the width of the line being printed on the paper. But over time, that changed. The small difference began to grow and grow until the new printout no longer even resembled the old. That 0.000127 initial difference was like the air generated from a butterfly's wing, as Lorenz saw it, yielding a tornado of change.

As a result, the *butterfly effect* is a way to describe how small changes can lead to big differences. More precisely, the butterfly effect refers to the way in which a slight difference or alteration in the original conditions of certain kinds of systems, like weather, can have major consequences over time.[2] In some situations, such as rolling a marble around in a bowl, a slight change in the beginning does not make much difference in the end; the

1. Lorenz, "Predictability," 72.

2. See Lorenz, "Butterfly Effect." The term *butterfly effect*, according to Lorenz, was coined by James Gleick in his book *Chaos*, whose account of the computer model incident I have relied upon here.

marble ends up at the bottom of the bowl. Differences in the initial condition of the marble's release in the bowl will be leveled out—the marble ends up at the bottom of the bowl no matter where in the bowl it is released.[3] But others systems are more dynamic. A minor change in the beginning is not leveled out in the end; instead change builds upon itself and accumulates and grows exponentially through time.

In the decades since Lorenz identified it, the idea of the butterfly effect has itself spread and led to whole new movements of scientific thought focusing upon chaos and complexity. Despite its name, chaos theory does not claim that disorder is at the heart of reality or that chaos is somehow the final word about the universe. The claim is, however, that even simple actions and structures can give rise to complex ones. From a naïve point of view, the phenomenon may seem chaotic, that is, unpredictable, but this has more to do with the limits of our understanding. The dynamics involved are so much more complicated or subtle than our means of measuring, symbolizing, or representing the reality we are trying to predict. Therefore, the "chaos" of chaos theory is more directly about our ability to know, especially our ability to measure and predict the impact of even the slightest flap of change.

Such a point, all by itself, is a major lesson about our capacity to know. But additionally, the butterfly effect may be a helpful way to think about the kinds of changes that occur in the cognitive abilities of hominids—a cobble tool or spark here, a whistle or a rhythm there. Neither Lucy nor you nor I could have foreseen the nuclear reactors or Grateful Dead concerts coming in time. Whatever differences first existed between our hominid ancestors and other apes may have been infinitesimal, not even visible on the primate printout. But over time, under certain conditions, we could be left wondering whether we are even looking at the same graph.

Here then may be a way to address the question of human uniqueness.

3. Gleik, *Chaos*, 48.

12

Originality, Time, and Education

How original are humans? The question flows throughout this book, sometimes explicitly, sometimes resting tacitly beneath a variety of reflections and discussions. In truth, the question hovers around any field of study having anything to do with human beings, whether studying behaviors, societies, psychology, philosophy, medicine, or even religion. Will a drug that arrests cancer in rats do the same in humans? Are dolphins naming each other as people do? What constitutes genuine tool-making? Do other creatures have culture? Are we alone made in the image of God? Do other creatures have souls? In short, how should we think about humanity in relation to the rest of the world? How original are we in relation to other animals, mammals, or primates even?

Of course, it depends. Answers pivot upon the realms of reality we consider, and at what level. In some ways humans are unique, in others not at all. We breathe oxygen and have eyes like so many land and air creatures, we build cathedrals and make movies like none other. In general, we are more like butterflies than stars, but we are even more like chimps than butterflies, more like *Australopithecus afarensis* (Lucy) than chimps, and more like other *Homo sapiens* than Lucy. By studying the bodies, the visible behaviors, or the remains of these various creatures we can go a long way in sorting out what's unique and what's not.

But what about the realm of knowing? What about the less visible territory of thinking and imagination, of cognition and consciousness? What about these more hidden realms of the mind and heart? Should we think of ourselves along a simple cognitive continuum with other creatures—apes particularly—employing the same cognitive skills like communication or tool use but extending them in new ways with our big heads? Are we just more of the same? Are our minds the same only on a larger scale? Or perhaps it would be better to admit that, when it comes to our mental abilities, we are indeed thoroughly unique in the animal world, not only in the sense that every species is unique, but uniquely unique. Perhaps the primate mind passed through some kind of phase shift or tipping point in humanity. Just as water becomes vapor with one degree of difference in temperature, so perhaps the waters of the primate mind arrived at a boiling point with *Homo sapiens*, the knowing human. If every species is unique and special in its own way, is there something extra special about humanity?

Sorting out the question of uniqueness in the realm of knowing is complicated indeed. Making matters worse is the fact that we have to rely on the very cognitive powers we are trying to understand to do so. A strange loop—knowing turns back around on itself like a snake swallowing its own tail.

The Wellspring of Originality

So how original are we? Are we uniquely unique?

Historically much theological reflection, based on the Bible, has answered yes—*there is something uniquely unique about humanity*. After all, we were made in God's own image and given dominion over the animals—so are we not the *crown of creation*? Creation is special, but we are especially special.

In this tradition the uniqueness of humanity carries large theological freight.[1] Human beings are closer to the Creator and have immortal souls that transcend our bodies; therefore, at the table of creation we are given the seat of honor. Animals have instincts; humans have God. In this view, human uniqueness is all tangled up with a certain religious view of the world as well as of the self, and my hunch is that here hide the real stakes in debates about evolution and creationism or biblical literalism. We want/need to feel special. Why

But the human-as-special represents only one school of theological thought. There is another, one also based upon the Bible, one not in such

---

1. See Pannenberg, *Anthropology*, and Van Huyssteen, *Alone in the World*, for excellent summaries and discussions of the theological (as well as philosophical and scientific) importance of the idea of human uniqueness.

a hurry to coronate humanity. In the same stories of Genesis we can read that humans are made from the dust of the earth—created. As created, humanity shares common origins with animals and earth, not to mention the sun and moon and heavens surrounding us. As many biblical scholars point out, biblically speaking the crown of creation is not humanity, but the Sabbath, the seventh day, when the Creator rested and we are commanded to do likewise. That which was created in six days, as Abraham Heschel points out in his book on the Sabbath, is *good*, but the seventh day God made *holy*.[2]

A careful reading of Genesis, then, reveals that a day—even time itself—is made sacred. Biblically speaking, we could say that humanity may be special but, frankly, time is even more special, "like an eternal burning bush," writes Heschel. "Though each instant must vanish to open the way to the next one, time itself is not consumed."[3] In effect, time is the wellspring of originality, making each thing in each moment unique.

In one sense, all types of creatures, by definition, are unique—strange—when compared to others. All species vary from one another in anatomy, genetic makeup, cognitive abilities, life expectancies, reproductive strategies and more. If they showed no differences, they would not be considered a different species. On the other hand, all creatures share some qualities of life; humans, jellyfish, butterflies, and microscopic viruses alike occupy space and endure for a finite amount of time. We could add plants and rocks and stars to this list as well. But of course the amount of space and time each takes up varies widely, not to mention what happens therein. Plants, stars, mosquitoes, and humans are qualitatively different from each other in many other ways. But taking the logic further, each individual star or mosquito or jellyfish or human is a complete original by the sheer fact of existing in a particular place for a particular time. Every moment—every moment within all moments—is an original.

Time generates originality. And because every moment is an original, paradoxically, time makes originality relative.

Time and Knowing

In an evolutionary worldview, time, albeit in a different way, is also something of an ever-vanishing, never-consumed bush. Opening its ways, as we

2. Heschel, *Sabbath*, 75.

3. Ibid., 229.

have seen, opens ambiguities about everything from tool use and communication to questions concerning the role of skull size in hominid species. The question of our uniqueness is not simple here in evolutionary time either.

Through seven million years, hominids have certainly developed some qualitative differences from their great ape cousins. The ways we live, how we think, and what we do to our habitat have parallels in other species, but, for example, the cognitive differences between searching for termites with a stick and searching space with the Hubble telescope are massive. From screeches and howls to alphabets and novels, from playful chasing and tumbling to the Olympic Games, the contrasts are too dramatic to gloss over.

Yet, when it comes to our genetics, we are only about as different from our chimpanzee cousins as lions are from tigers, or as mice are from rats.[4] Our biological differences from other great apes pale when compared to the cultural and cognitive ones, as if our bodies lived by a different evolutionary clock. As Michael Tomasello puts it, when it comes to evolution and the human mind, we have a time problem: "The fact is, there simply has not been enough time for normal processes of biological evolution involving genetic variation and natural selection to have created, one by one, each of the cognitive skills necessary for modern humans to invent and maintain complex tool-use industries and technologies, complex forms of symbolic communication and representation, and complex social organizations and institutions."[5]

This time problem reveals yet another version of a mind-body problem, that is, how can we be so similar biologically, bodily, to other primates and so different cognitively, mentally? And how could have all these differences have developed so relatively rapidly, especially when most of them seem to have emerged in the last couple hundred thousand years, if not more recently? In the realm of biological change and evolution, time flows like a glacier; but in the culture and behaviors of humanity time seems to flow more like a mighty river, if not a laser.

What is it about humans that accounts for such dramatic differences? Could there be some cognitive capacity or ability that functionally took the speed of development out of the slow-moving time of biological change and moved it into the relatively rapid transformations of historical-cultural

4. Tomasello, *Cultural Origins*, 2.
5. Ibid.

time? After all, with the same basic body we can travel by foot, by horse, by car, jet, or rocket alike. We can communicate with gestures, spoken words, or writing, through the telegraph, telephone, or the Internet, with the same basic biological equipment. Was there some slight change in the species—a fractional difference on the biological continuum with other primates that, in time, generated a butterfly effect?

The short answer is yes. Education is the key.

What Did You Learn Today?

Teaching and learning in humans generates a butterfly effect. While other creatures can learn from each other, humans manage not only to learn, but to accumulate what they learn; they build upon and pass along a good portion of learning from generation to generation. Changes in cultural practices and patterns of life, changes in ideas and language, can accelerate without the need for comparably large biological changes. Technologies and institutions can become more and more complex, and societies can generate new ideas and practices by utilizing such accumulated knowledge. Education—from the simplest forms of learning words at home to complex school systems and university curricula—is at the heart of this cascade of knowledge that leads to such dramatic lifestyle differences from our close genetic cousins.

To be more precise, as Michael Tomasello helps explain, when we talk about education we are referring to a form of *social learning* or *cultural transmission*, something that is *not* unique to our species. Other animals can and do learn from their peers. "Cultural transmission includes such things as fledgling birds mimicking their species-typical song from parents, rat pups eating only the foods eaten by their mothers, ants locating food by following the pheromone trails of conspecifics, young chimpanzees learning the tool-use practices of the adults around them, and human children acquiring the linguistic conventions of others in their social groups."[6] In short, cultural transmission itself is relatively common in the creaturely world, especially in animals that rely upon some form of nurture or care of the young (birds, rats) or social organization (ants) for survival. Cultural transmission can be highly useful in a species because it allows individual creatures to take advantage of the knowledge that already exists and skills that have already been figured out, and helps them avoid at least some of

6. Ibid., 4.

the pitfalls and potential dangers along the way.[7] So, cultural transmission itself is not unique to humanity; we clearly rest on the continuum with other species that learn from their elders and companions.

But if this is true, the issue still remains: Why haven't birds or chimps or rats developed their own equivalent of novels and symphonies, telescopes or cars? Why have chimps, as far as we can tell, not accumulated more knowledge or developed more complex tools over the last couple million years? There seem to be no parallels to cave paintings or hand axes to be found among other primates, let alone stained glass windows or nuclear fusion. In other words, cultural transmission may be necessary, but alone it is insufficient to account for the scale of differences between humans and other species.

Because of this Tomasello suggests that there is a *species-unique* mode of cultural transmission that allows, what he calls, a *ratchet effect* in cultural transmission. Think of it as cultural transmission with a twist. The twist is whatever it is that enables our species to pool, accumulate, and modify knowledge and practices over time in ways that other species do not.[8] Let's say three million years ago a chimp uses a broken cobble to crack open a nut. Three million years later, sometimes chimps, now and then, here and there, use a cobble to crack open a nut. But for Lucy's descendants, over time, the cobble becomes a tool for chopping bones as well as nuts, and is then sharpened into an axe or knife that can in turn be thrown or placed on a stick and improved by using other materials, some of which make sparks, which in turn can be controlled to make fires to stay warm in cold climates, allowing our ancestors to cook a greater variety of foods, and so it goes. Rather than a song here or a pheromone trail there, human cultural transmission is more like the flap of a butterfly's wings in Brazil generating a tornado in Texas.

This is a form of *cumulative* cultural transmission requiring not only creativity or innovation but, as Tomasello points out, something more, something that helps retain or stabilize the innovation. For cultural transmission to become cumulative, a species must have not only some creative capacities but also have strong imitative abilities to keep the innovation alive long enough to become part of the group. Whatever the helpful innovation is—say using a rock to chop open bones for marrow—it has to be imitated by others, and done often enough to preserve the new behavior over time.

7. Ibid.
8. Ibid., 4–5.

A species good at imitation is more likely to preserve the behavior over time. A species like chimps may be wonderfully ingenious at figuring out how to fish for termites with a stick or meeting all sorts of challenges in the environment, but if they are not great imitators, the clever innovation may die out quickly and never become stabilized within the group.

About this, Tomasello echoes a point made by Jane Goodall, who believes that a lot of creative acts in fact do happen among primates (other than humans). The problem is that unless someone (like Goodall) is watching constantly, these innovations are missed. Why? They are random, individual, and not imitated enough to be preserved by the group.[9] Essentially other apes may be "too cool for school." That is, in their natural habitats over the past few million years, they have been sufficiently clever and did perfectly well without a lot of need to imitate.

To be clear, other apes can and do learn from each other, can and do imitate. Groups and regions of apes can and do demonstrate cultural differences, that is, different patterns of behaviors that each group sustains over time to a limited degree. For example, in East Africa chimps may fish for termites with skinny sticks threaded into termite mounds, but in West Africa chimps are more likely to take a big stick and simply smash the mounds and then scoop up the termites with their hands. Does this mean West African chimps are more aggressive or even violent? No. Instead, it likely implies that each habitat lends itself to each behavior—in West Africa the mounds are made of softer dirt; the East African mounds are much more difficult to break up.[10]

The implication is that, first of all, particular habitats play a large role even in chimp social learning. Chimps will learn from each other, and do so even at a large enough scale to be noticed (by humans) as a group behavior; but it helps if the environment is abundantly rich with opportunities for the innovative behavior to be repeated over and over again (for example loaded with termite mounds and sticks). Otherwise the practice is less likely to be preserved by the group over time. And in fact often these practices do rise and fall within a generation of chimps. They are culturally fragile.

Compare this to the fact that humans create extremely complex social institutions (like school systems, governments, religious organizations, financial markets and so much more) to help sustain culturally transmitted

---

9. Ibid. 39. Tomasello himself is referring to Goodall, *Chimpanzees*, and Kummer and Goodall, "Innovative Behaviour."

10. Tomasello, *Cultrual Origins*, 28.

knowledge, practices, and patterns of behavior. (And it may be no accident that all of these realms struggle within themselves between innovation and imitation, between creativity and sustainability, between progress and conservation.) While our cultural knowledge may feel fragile to many of us—we may bemoan the loss of wisdom and knowledge carried by our elders—relative to the cultural knowledge of other species, this is nothing. Then again, our ways of life depend so much more upon accumulated knowledge.

In general, then, cultural transmission is important territory for addressing the question of human uniqueness, our originality as knowers. Cultural transmission puts us in continuity with other species that learn from each other, yet it opens the possibility that there may be a particularly human form of learning that allows us to accumulate this knowledge over time and through the generations so that the knowledge we gain can also be retained. This in turn would help account for the dramatic differences between a stick in a termite mound and sticking an oil rig into the earth, even as the underlying dynamic of tool use is at work in each.

Cumulative cultural transmission—let's call it cumulative knowledge—stands on the threshold between the slow-moving time of biological evolution and the relatively rapid pace of historical time. Once again we can notice timelines within timelines, and we live in all of them. Our bodies reflect millions of years of gradual change while our cultures and forms of knowledge, by comparison, change at lightning speed. Cumulative knowledge, education, and teaching and learning bridge us to our deep past even while accounting for the ways we stand on the other side of the river of knowledge alone.

Yet, Not Yet

Education is key, yet a question remains: how do we accumulate knowledge?

We can point to the ways in which we learn and build upon learning and see the signs of uniqueness, but in truth, this only backs the issue up a little further. We are still left wondering what enables us to accumulate knowledge. Balancing creativity with stability seems important at the level of social groups, but what about at the individual level? Is there something about our minds that makes a species-unique form of cultural transmission or education possible? Is there some capacity or ability that in Lucy would have been hardly distinguishable from other apes?

What we are looking for is an equivalent, in the realm of knowing, to a few extra decimal points in the cognitive life of our ancestors.

13

Blueberry Picking

EDUCATION—THIS PECULIAR HUMAN ABILITY to accumulate cultural knowledge through the generations—gets us closer to understanding how a slight difference between hominids and other great apes could have generated a butterfly effect over time. But the question remains: How do we accumulate knowledge? What's going on in human knowers that they can indeed learn so much so quickly from the generations before and build upon that knowledge in ways that we do not see in other primates? What bit of discontinuity in the hominid mind allowed the ratcheting of knowledge?

It is tempting to point to our use of full-blown symbolic, grammatical, recursive language as the key (as many do), since we certainly do use our words to pass along know-how, wisdom, stories, songs, books, manuals, and whole libraries of information to others.[1] And I have no doubt that language has provided an extra large crank in the ratcheting—at first orally, then with writing and books and computers as well—helping us accumulate even more rapidly the knowledge that goes before us.

But in the end I suspect the key is older than words. I suspect something in us allowed sounds to become words in the first place—perhaps the

1. Steven Mithen, for example, speculates that language generated what he calls "cognitive fluidity" in the minds of our early *Homo sapien* ancestors—differentiating us from the Neanderthals (and all other preceding hominids). He imagines the mind as a kind of cathedral with multiple chapels, containing a variety of intelligences—social, technical, and natural-historical, for example. Before language, these were self-contained chapels, with thick walls between them. But with syntactical language the walls broke down between these intelligences, yielding new realms of creativity and imagination. Mithen, *Prehistory*, 71. See Mithen, *Singing Neanderthals*, especially ch. 16, for a good summary of cognitive fluidity. See also Van Huyssteen, *Alone*, 193ff., for a discussion of cognitive fluidity in relation to human uniqueness and the religious imagination.

reason humans were ever able to develop languages at all, even the ability that continues to allow language to take root and grow among children today. Following the work of several thoughtful scholars of cognition, I suspect the key is tied up with *mind reading*.[2]

What Are Your Intentions?

Imagine that you and I are taking a walk on a nice summer day, let's say in the Ontario wilderness. We are chatting about our jobs or children or the state of the economy—or all of the above—but as we are walking and talking I point to a bush. On the bush you can see beautiful ripe blueberries. Without missing a beat in the conversation we both go to the bush and start picking the fruit.

Maybe we had set out to pick blueberries, maybe not; perhaps it was just a walk and a visit. That simple act of pointing, however, allowed you to read my mind. Obviously, not in some kind of science fiction, telepathic, ESP sort of way, but in a wordless act that directed your attention and let you know what I was thinking nonetheless.

First of all, the gesture directed your attention toward the bush with the beautiful blueberries. I could have said, without pointing or turning my head, "Look over to your left about 45 degrees, between the giant granite boulder—the one approximately 15 feet away—the one with a pink spot at the top. Between it and the dead pine tree broken in half—the one to the left of the boulder—you will see a blueberry bush with ripe berries and we should go over and pick them." Or I could say nothing at all about the blueberries, and point. If you know anything at all about blueberries or if you know I love blueberries, you will be able to read my mind—or more precisely, to read my intentions.

Or, in a slightly more complex situation: Perhaps I hate blueberries but you love them. I saw you eating them the day before, with delight, when we found a blueberry bush on our walk yesterday. So you know that I know that you love them. You know I hate them. But when I point, you would still be able to read my intentions: *there are some ripe blueberries; let's pick some*

2. There is a rich intellectual tradition of mind/intention reading going back at least to Act Psychology and early phenomenology of the late 19th century. One of the best recent discussions of the role of "mind reading" in experimental psychology is Tomasello, et al., "Understanding and Sharing Intentions." The "Open Peer Commentary" section includes review and discussion of the target article by over 50 other scholars representing a wide range of relevant fields, as well as a response from the authors.

for you. In fact, not only are you reading my intentions, the simple gesture that at first directed your attention and allowed you to read my mind, easily allows us to share the intention, to share in the desire to pick blueberries. *My* goal becomes *our* goal. Even more, this pointing and mind reading could conceivably have happened without any words at all, not only on our walk today, but on one that took place a million years ago, maybe two or three million even.

Experiments in Mind Reading

In general, when compared to other species, humans are particularly good at such mind reading, at discerning the intentions of others. Experimental psychologists have devised many clever ways to test such mind reading in children and other primates, but a typical way involves an adult "trying" to do something and failing. For example, an adult holds out a toy or rattle or pacifier to a baby. Perhaps the child reaches for the object, but the adult is unyielding, or worse, takes it away completely. Frankly, the baby is being teased with the object. Not surprisingly, this upsets the child; and she will start frowning or crying, or she will simply turn her gaze away from the adult or the object.

On the other hand—and this is the revealing part of the experiment— if the adult "accidently" drops the object on the way to handing it to the child, if the adult seems to be making a good-faith effort to hand over the object, the baby exhibits much more patience. She will wait longer, not frown or cry, but wait out the efforts of the clumsy researcher. In other words, the child seems to be able to read the intention of the adult—that he wants or is trying to give the object over to her.[3]

There are many varieties of such experiments but the general developmental picture for human babies is this: for the first six to nine months of life it doesn't matter whether the adult is "trying" to hand over the object or not—babies exhibit the same impatience either way. But somewhere between 9 and 12 months children can differentiate teasing or withholding from what appears to be clumsy behavior; they show more patience with accidental dropping or other disruptions that seem to be unintentional.[4] In other words, one-year-olds are beginning to read the minds of others. They understand that others are trying to do something, that others have

3. See Capenter et al., "Social Cognition."

4. Tomasello et al., "Understanding and Sharing Intentions," 679.

intentions, and that these intentions can result in actions that bring delight or frustration.

Of course the children are getting clues from the bodies of others—arm positions and movements, eye contact, and head direction, for example—so perhaps *mind reading* is more accurately called *body reading*. But, significantly, these children are beginning to learn there is something invisible behind the visible cues—a goal, a desire, a purpose, an attitude, a motivation, an intention that organizes and gives direction to the behavior of a body. So even by one year of age, most children are beginning to appreciate that invisible forces give rise to visible actions.

What about other primates? To what extent, if any, can they read minds, bodies, or gestures?

Chimps in particular perform similarly to one-year-old humans when it comes to "trying." That is, they too show more patience with an adult (human) who seems to be trying to give them a desired object (like food) but appears to be clumsy. They get upset much more quickly if the adult seems to be intentionally withholding or teasing.[5] So, it appears that great apes in general, including young humans, understand intentions. They too are reading invisible motivations from visible bodily cues.

In short, great apes—not only humans—can appreciate that others have intentions, and in this sense they are mind readers. So, mind reading alone does not seem to be the flap of difference that allows human beings to accumulate knowledge in such cyclonic ways. But we are getting closer. Intentions can get more complicated than these simple one-on-one interactions. Even pointing to a blueberry bush may present a larger challenge than one would think.

The Point of Pointing

Another set of experiments may shine some good light on this matter of intentions and reveal more precisely what humans are particularly good at in relation to mind reading. These experiments, like our blueberry-picking walk, also involve pointing and food, but, in this case, are more like a version of the old pea-and-shell game of hucksters and magicians.[6]

5. Tomasello, *Human Communication*, 46ff. See also Tomasello et al. "Understanding and Sharing Intentions."

6. Tomasello et al., "Comprehension." See also Tomasello, *Human Communication*, 38ff.; and Tomasello et al.,"Understanding and Sharing Intentions," 724–25, for more recent interpretations of the results.

Imagine that in front of you are three containers, let's say buckets, and inside one and only one of the buckets is a prize. If you guess the correct bucket, you get the prize. The beauty is that, as an experiment, this scenario can be created for apes or humans alike. And this is what Michael Tomasello and his colleagues did.

In the pea-and-shell game the pea is shown resting beneath one of the shells. Then the shells are shuffled around to present the challenge of finding it. But in this experiment, a curtain is drawn between the subject and the buckets, so the subject does not know where the experimenter (let's call her the "hider") puts the prize. The curtain is opened and it's time to guess. And of course, with no other information, subjects will guess correctly, on average, about a third of the time.

For the nonhuman subjects (some chimps, some orangutans), the prize is food, and they have learned (from previous conditioning) that only one bucket has food. And they have learned that they only get one try at finding it. For the human subjects (two- and three-year-olds) the prize is a sticker. So, while the curtain conceals the buckets, the hider places the prize in one of them. The curtain is opened and it is time to choose. This is the basic setup for the experiment.

The twist in this setup is that another researcher is standing behind the hider (let's call him the "snitch"). After the curtain is opened, the hider looks away for a moment to write something down. At that point the snitch quietly tilts the correct bucket so that the subject can see where the prize is. When the hider—now looking up again—invites the children or apes to choose, they of course choose the container with the prize. No surprise here—it did not matter whether the subject was human, the results were virtually the same (except for one forgetful orangutan who chose the wrong container three times out of the 18 tries). In fact this part of the experiment is really just a warm-up to help the children and apes play the game and learn that the snitch is their helper in this game. The real test is yet to come.

In another set of rounds, when the hider is looking away, the snitch does not tilt the container to reveal the prize. Instead, this time, he simply points to the correct bucket (the snitch was on the same side of the curtain as the hider, so saw where she hid the prize.) So what happens in this situation?

All the children understood the gesture, and therefore chose the right container. The apes did not.

The chimps and orangutans alike would look at the snitch, make eye contact, follow the pointing, even look at the container being pointed at, but then more often than not, choose another container, as if the snitch had not done a thing. In the words of the researchers, it's as if the chimp/orangutan thinks, "There's a bucket. That's boring. Where's the food?"[7] While the children understood the point of pointing, the other great apes did not. What's going on?

It could be that the chimps and orangutans simply did not understand the human gesture. After all, in the wild these great apes don't point. The gesture would be as meaningless as wiggling your ears. They did not have to understand much when the snitch simply revealed the food directly—they saw the food and remembered.

But the problem with this explanation is that nonhuman great apes raised around humans do seem to understand pointing. They will follow your arm and head movements and look where you point, just as those in the experiment looked at the buckets. In some cases, great apes have even learned to point themselves, at least for humans. They will look into your eyes, point (or more like reach) for some food, and thereby make a request. Apparently they have learned that humans may actually respond to such requests (and not simply take the food for themselves).[8]

So, given half a chance, great apes can learn some gestures and the intent behind them. This is less surprising given that even in the wild great apes themselves do use some gestures (other than pointing) to communicate intentions. For example, chimps will raise their arms to initiate play or put their backs in another's face to invite grooming. Remarkably, sometimes they will even improvise if at first a gesture does not work. If raising an arm fails to engage the other chimp in play, then the chimp may throw something at the other chimp to get her attention and try again. In short, chimps appreciate whether others are paying attention or not, and they even attempt, with gestures, to affect those states of another's attention.[9]

---

7. Tomasello et al., "Understanding and Sharing Intentions," 724. To be clear, this particular experiment is only one illustration of many that have yielded similar results.

8. Tomasello, *Human Communication*, 35.

9. Ibid., ch. 2. According to Tomasello, compared to primate vocalization, primate gestures are more flexible and complex. Primate vocalizations tend to be more tightly bound to emotional states—shrieks of alarm or threatening grunts, for example. The same is true for most gestures as well—facial expressions and chest pounding, for example. But there are a few gestures, especially among other (nonhuman) great apes— chimps, bonobos, gorillas, and orangutans—that are used in less emotionally intense situations, for example, in play or in grooming. If gestures are more flexible, they could mean more than one thing.

Nonhuman great apes, in other words, use gestures "in the impera-tive," as Tomasello puts it, to get another to do something—for example, to give up some food, to play, or to groom.[10] In the wild chimps do sometimes beg and reach for food that another ape has in its possession. But there is one thing they do not do: *they do not point to a third location.* They do not point in order to request that another ape go get the food. We can speculate that in the wild pointing to food would likely not work out so well. Drawing another's attention to the food would actually lower the odds that the food would then wind up with the pointer. If you and I are chimps and I point to some food, you may get there first and I may be left hungry.

To summarize: great apes—human or otherwise—can use and under-stand gestures; great apes can read the attention and intentions of others. And yet, we still have this situation: when the snitch points to the bucket with food, chimps and orangutans will look, but they do not connect the pointing with the hidden food. They do not seem to understand that the snitch is trying to help. Two-year-old humans do.

The implication seems to be that the chimps and orangutans could understand that the snitch wanted them to look at a particular bucket, so they looked, but this is as far as the mind reading went. These apes did not seem to understand that the snitch was intending to help them find the food, even though the snitch helped them do so in the previous rounds. They did not read the intent to help in the snitch's pointing; they may not have even realized that the snitch was intending to help them in the first rounds, when tilting the bucket. They simply learned where the food was (and perhaps did not even think about the intentions of the snitch). The children, however, immediately interpreted the point to reveal the inten-tions of the snitch to help them find the stickers.

The key difference, in the researchers' words, is that "the infant knows that she and the adult are playing a hiding-finding game: the child's role is to find the toy, and the adult's role is to help her. So when the adult points to one of the buckets, the child immediately sees this as relevant to this game and the adult's role in it. . . . The chimpanzee, in contrast, does not understand the collaborative structure of the game."[11]

In all, it appears that great apes use and understand some gestures, especially in relation to requests—*give me, play with me, groom me.* But when it comes to *informing—I am pointing because you will be interested;*

---

10. Tomasello *Human Communication*, 34ff.

11. Tomasello et al., "Understanding and Sharing Intentions," 724.

the food you want is over there—understanding seems to come to a halt unless you are human.[12]

And there is no evidence that any primates but humans point just to share the view—*look at that beautiful sunset with me* or *look at that glittering rock over there; isn't that something?* Humans point, gesture, communicate, talk, write, and more, as often as not, just to share the experience. Not only the literal view, but also the emotions evoked, and the memories shared of life together.

Sharing

What a very slight difference here. In some cases great apes can read the intentions of others. If I am trying to hand some food to a chimp or a one-year-old baby, either will show patience if I am clumsy and show frustration if I tease. They both seem to understand my intentions and respond accordingly. If I point to a bucket, chimps and babies alike will look—they seem to understand my intention (that I want them to look) and respond accordingly. But when adding one extra step, one extra layer of intention—*I want you to look because you will find the prize*—the chimps and orangutans hit the limits of their mind-reading abilities while human two-year-olds show no trouble at all. In fact, humans are able to do so soon after their first birthday.[13]

Children can read the *intent behind the intent.* In the experiment, pointing contained not one but two intents:

Intent 1: *Look at that bucket.*

Intent 2: *Find the prize.*

Does this extra little step in mind reading get us any closer to that slight breeze of difference between ourselves and other primates—a flap of a fragile wing that could, over enough time, lead to a whirlwind of cultural change? Those who conducted these experiments answer yes. Based upon hundreds of comparative studies between children and nonhuman primates they conclude that although other great apes "have human-like skills

---

12. Tomasello *Human Communication*, 87.

13. Tomasello et al., "Understanding and Sharing intentions," 724.

for understanding individual intentionality, they do not have human-like skills and motivations of shared intentionality."[14]

The truth is, in addition to the two intents identified above, there is yet another intent hidden in the snitch's point, one that puts the pointing in context:

Intent 3: *I am trying to help you find the prize.*

The child wants to get stickers. The hider wants to conceal stickers and make it more difficult for the child to reach her goal. But the snitch wants the same thing as the child wants—not to get stickers for himself; he wants the child to get stickers. The child and the snitch share the exact same goal. Remarkably, the child understands this. The child realizes that the snitch is trying to help her get stickers. Thus a "shared," or "we," or "joint" intention is born.

If we can share in a common intention, new possibilities emerge for all kinds of collaborative activities. Why? Because we can submit our individual intentions to the shared one and, in turn, make all kinds of adjustments in light of the other. For example, if we share the intention of moving a heavy log across a field, we could each start to push the log, rolling it in the same direction. We could coordinate our rolls to keep the log on a straight route, or we could even each pick up an end and coordinate our steps to carry the log together. If you are walking a little faster than I am, I can speed up or you can slow down, or we each do a little of both. Dozens of micro-adjustments can be made in service to the joint intention of moving the log. Yet, as Tomasello remarks, based upon hundreds of studies of primate behavior, nonhuman great apes simply don't do this. "In general," he says, "it is almost unimaginable that two chimpanzees might spontaneously do something as simple as carry something heavy together or make a tool together."[15]

The trick to collaboration is that I have to know you want the same thing I want, and you have to know that I want the same thing you want. The joint intention "contains both self and other." A joint intention "requires that each participant cognitively represent both roles of the collaboration in a single representational format—holistically, from a 'bird's-eye view,' as it were—thus enabling role reversal and mutual helping."[16] The bird's-eye

14. Tomasello, *Human Communication*, 181.
15. Ibid., 176.
16. Tomasello et al., "Understanding and Sharing Intentions," 681.

view sees my intent and your intent at the same time. When we both take a bird's-eye perspective, then we both see that we both see. More simply put, we both know that we both know that we are trying to move the log. And because of that we can work together, even without thinking much about it.

In summary, great apes are good mind readers, probably because they are such social creatures. They can read the basic intentions of others and adjust their behavior accordingly. They even, at times, try to affect the intentions of others through gestures—*play with me, give me, groom me*. Great apes of the human variety seem to have taken the social life and extended it even to the realm of intentions behind intentions. We put our intentions in relation to each other. We put our minds together. We can take a bird's-eye view on the situation, allowing each of us to stand in the intentions of the other as well as our own all at the same time.

Hyper-Social

As impressive as the ability to collaborate is—to put our minds together, to engage in the pursuit of joint goals—the fact that we want to do so is equally amazing. Initiate a simple game of rolling a ball back and forth with a one-year-old and she will quickly catch on and play the game, and for no other reward than to play with you. Sit and look at a book together, play Peekaboo or Paddy Cake or make funny faces at each other. Stop abruptly and the child will try to re-engage you in the shared activity. Walk down a sidewalk and he will point to shiny gum wrappers or an airplane or a dandelion because he wants you to see it too.

The ability to take a bird's-eye view that is aware of self and other at the same time seems to be more than a raw ability, it is a desire as well, a desire to share experiences. So we point and collaborate and inform and make games and more. Compared to other primates, we are hyper-social. We delight in sharing visible and invisible spaces alike.

Pinpointing precisely when and why we took this hyper-social turn within the last six or seven million years may be impossible to determine. But it is difficult to resist seeing early signs of it in the tool-making traditions between two and three million years ago. These choppers and flakes and axes may be our earliest visible tokens of shared activities. What may have begun as a purely functional tool hit upon by accident (much like a stick is discovered to be good for drawing termites from a hole) may have taken on new significance when someone intentionally showed another how to make one, or when they gave it away or shared it. Sharing the tool or sharing the knowledge at work in the tool—either may have sent us down the human road of sharing intentions.

Another possibility is in food sharing. Perhaps a few particularly generous or helpful hominids began sharing some food with each other, opening up new possibilities in cooperation and therefore new possibilities for our minds. "What might be selected for in these tolerant, peacefully co-feeding individuals" writes Tomasello, "is the ability to create joint goals and joint attention."[17] If I know we are going to share the blueberries, then I don't mind pointing to them and directing your attention to the bush and working together to pick them.

Then again (thinking like a drummer), perhaps it was rhythm. As our earliest drumming ancestors synchronized the production of sound with one another, maybe they were learning their first lessons in synchronizing intentions—micro-adjustments here and there in relation to each other to create a delightful, shared experience of rhythm.

The point of the point is that we can share. We can share walks and talks, stories and concerns, delights and frustrations, and we can even share some blueberries. We can share our intentions to get something done; we can share them just to share them. These days we do a lot of such sharing through language, and language certainly extends our ability to read one another's minds (I can tell you what I am thinking); but I am persuaded, for now, that language has grown in the soil of mind reading and not the other way around.[18] We can read intentions without the involvement of language, whereas we cannot understand language without reading intentions.

Sharing What We Know

When the ability to read the intentions behind intentions combines with the desire to share them, we have the seeds of a powerful mind. First of all, the ability to appreciate invisible forces at all puts us on the road to understand the world around us, including other people, in deeper ways. We can understand that people act out of intents and desires. But we can also appreciate that such intents and desires are at work in other animals as

17. Tomasello, *Human Communication*, 194.

18. This in fact is the case being made in Tomasello et al., "Understanding and Sharing Intentions," and Tomasello, *Human Communication*.

well, and if we understand them a little better, we could be more successful in hunting, for example, or not being hunted.

We may even begin to appreciate that hidden forces are at work in other arenas of the physical environment—in the weather and trees and flowing rivers, for example. If we see lightning strike a tree and make it burn, we may begin to wonder about the intentions behind the event and the relationships between lightning, wood, smoke, and fire. We may even want to share those intentions and make fire ourselves. In short, our deepened understanding of social relationships may have led to our deepened understanding of relationships in the physical environment.[19] Our hypersocial minds may have led the way to fire making and the field of physics alike. Seeing beneath the surface of life to the invisible forces at work—whether in other people, in other creatures, or in the skies—indeed makes for a powerful form of understanding.

Yet, initially, it seems this powerful mind began as only a few decimal points worth of difference from our great ape relatives. One small step of intention reading in the cognitive life, one giant leap for the species. We can share intentions to get things done; we can share them to share experiences; we can share knowledge; we can inform. Sharing intentions is the key to cumulative knowledge, to education. Sharing intentions is the gentle flap of a butterfly's wings generating the slightest breeze of difference at first, but over time, leading to some tornadic differences in the human knower.

This would account for the ways in which we could be original knowers yet so similar to other great apes all at the same time. We stand firmly in the community of creation, yet we do so with a unique ability to know. The origin of our original knowing rests in sharing.

& the future of humanity

---

19. See Tomasello, *Cultural Origins*, ch.1, for an excellent discussion of how humans came to understand mediating forces at work in the physical world based upon our social intelligence.

14

The Age of Religious Knowing

SOMEWHERE ALONG THE LINE our ancestors got religion. Just as they learned to read one another's minds, we now find ourselves reading the intentions of the cosmos. So what is the connection, if any, between original knowing and religious knowing? How far back does religion go? And despite all the bickering from within and criticisms from without, why does religion endure?

Such questions resist easy answers as the challenges are abundant. For one, no consensus exists about what religion even is. For another, we are once again reaching into a foggy past where it is all too tempting to misproject our present attitudes and beliefs back, especially about things invisible. Nonetheless, given the kind of minds we have—reading intentions behind intentions, seeing invisible forces at work in the visible world—how can we not ask?

The tree of knowledge is deceptively powerful.

Religion?

Over a hundred years ago, recognizing the difficulty of the subject matter, the psychologist-turned-philosopher of religion William James took an intentionally wide approach to religion in his Gifford Lectures. Attempting to describe the great "varieties of religious experience" in the broadest of terms, and not only the official versions of them, he suggested that the religious life "consists of the belief that there is an unseen order, and that our supreme good lies in harmoniously adjusting ourselves thereto. This belief and this adjustment are the religious attitude in the soul."[1] This religious attitude, as he described it, is a certain "sense of reality," a perception of "something there" that is irreducible to the bodily senses.[2] The religious life, for James, flows from an awareness of "more" and our desire to be in "union" with it.[3] Religion involves more than cognition of course, but even so, our knowing—perhaps especially the ability to read and share intentions—is deeply implicated.

In a much more recent approach, Pascal Boyer offers another description: "Religion is about the existence and causal powers of nonobservable entities and agencies. These may be one unique God or many different gods or spirits or ancestors, or a combination of these different kinds."[4] Boyer, like James, is looking for commonalities among what can be wildly diverse phenomena. As he reminds us, the notion of one supreme God is foreign to many religions. For some there may be two or more supreme divinities, and they may or may not seem to care much about the everyday affairs of people. In other religions—some forms of Buddhism for example—the gods themselves die or are caught in the cycle of reincarnation.[5] While some religions may focus upon salvation or liberation or faith as a major theme, others have little to say about such matters. Even among the major monotheistic religions—those emphasizing one God—hosts of spirits, saints, angels, demons, ghosts, witches, and jinn populate the religious imagination nonetheless.[6] If religion is anything, it is diverse.

The drawback of broad and general descriptions of religion is that they reduce the great variety to something like a lowest common denominator between all sorts of otherwise different beliefs, practices, attitudes, and expressions. And because such descriptions try to stand outside any particular religious perspective, they tend toward the abstract and chilly. It's hard to imagine the First Church of the Unseen Order and Nonobservable Entities ever making a splash.

Even so, even with these drawbacks, when something is so widespread around the planet—involving unseen realities, regular rituals, concern over life and death, beliefs about the cosmos, devotion, and shared

1. James, *Varieties*, 53.
2. Ibid., 58.
3. Ibid., 51.
4. Boyer, *Religion Explained*, 7.
5. Ibid., 9–10.
6. Ibid., 8-9.

practices—our curiosity will not easily brake. Despite the drawbacks, the benefit of a broad approach to religion rests in the possibility of seeing that the great varieties of religious experience actually share something very deep, something rooted in our common humanity, something old.

Interpreting Signs

Presuming our ancestors sensed some "there" there, some sense of "more," how far back does it go? What signs might suggest some kind of religious attitude of the soul, clues to a world populated with spirits or gods?

Burial practices and cave paintings of animals, for example, are frequent favorite signs of religion among prehistorians as theses practices strike chords with more contemporary religious ideas. Cave paintings reveal the ability for symbolic thought, "reflecting a mythological world" full of animal spirits and shamans; burial reflects a belief in a "transition to a non-physical form."[7] If we were to date religion on the basis of these, cave paintings go back about 30 thousand years in France and Spain, but there are signs of earlier, potentially symbolic art some 75 thousand years ago in South Africa.[8] The earliest burials could have been anywhere from 90 thousand years ago to as far back as 300 thousand years ago (depending upon how you interpret 27 skeletons clumped together in Atapuerca, Spain). So, paintings and burials occurred tens—if not hundreds—of thousands of years ago.

The challenge is interpretation. Since these potential signs of religious life occurred tens to hundreds of thousands of years before writing, let alone audio or visual recording, we can only imagine what they involved. Reading the intent behind the intent of a burial site or a cave painting is anything but simple. Burials could have been for hygienic or aesthetic purposes (who wants to watch a body rot, or smell it?). Cave paintings or animal totems could have been made for purely functional or instructional purposes (*here is what a bull looks like* or *watch out for bears*). Then again, these could, as some speculate, be tokens of belief in another world or animal gods; they could be signs of the religious attitude of our ancestors. On the one hand our prehistoric ancestors may not have had any wisp of anything like a religious attitude—any more than a chimp seems to (that we know of).

7. Mithen, *Prehistory*, 176.
8. The Blombos Cave excavation.

On the other, their thoughts may have been teeming with sprits and ghosts and more.

In truth, I am not confident we will ever know. Once again, large time frames open up large ambiguities.

Out of Context, Out of Mind

In a strange-loopy sort of way, our very ability to read minds—to read intents behind intents—creates both the desire to know and the ambiguity that gets in the way. For humans, understanding involves not only the surface of events, but what's going on behind the scenes. A point of the finger is more than a body movement, and this is why reading intentions matters so much. Our sense of the intent behind the intent provides the context for understanding. As Tomasello and his colleagues explain, "Understanding intentions is foundational because it provides the interpretive matrix for deciding precisely what it is that someone is doing in the first place. Thus the exact same physical movement may be seen as giving an object, sharing it, loaning it, moving it, getting rid of it, returning it, trading it, selling it, and on and on and on—depending on the goals and intentions of the actor."[9]

Whether someone is pointing to a bucket or to a blueberry bush, an interpretive matrix helps us understand what someone is doing and why. The same is true for understanding the meaning of a cave painting from 30 thousand years ago, a grave from 90 thousand years ago, a baptism today, a journey to Mecca, or an act of kindness. From within the interpretive matrix of religious belief—shared with others—the acts could be deeply meaningful and ways of "harmoniously adjusting" (as James put it) our lives in relation to the intentions of the universe. Outside such an interpretive matrix, however, such acts may be confusing, meaningless, silly, incomprehensible, or terribly misunderstood. Prehistoric acts and artifacts—as noted throughout this book—are particularly difficult to interpret precisely because we are so far removed from the actors. Even if they could read one another's intentions when they buried someone's body, we cannot be sure we can read theirs, now, accurately. Burial could have been a sign of belief in a next world, therefore a sign of religion as people often see it today. Then again fire could have been understood as gift from the gods; raindrops could have been spirits watering the ground. Burials, paintings,

9. Tomasello et al., "Understanding and Sharing Intentions," 675.

fire, rain, food, trees, dancing, drums, beads, tools, blueberries, butterflies, red birds, a jaguar, a quiet cave, a noisy wind, *aurora borealis*, or sharing a drink, for example, could have generated a sense of the "more" or not. We just don't know.

So what do we know?

Not much, until people began to write. What we do know is that as long as there has been history, the gods have been there. As long as people have been writing down words in songs and stories, and passing them along to the next generation, the gods have been involved. They have been sung to, prayed to, written about, feared, revered, and even given voice. And this has made it slightly easier to read the intentions and beliefs of our ancestors for the past few thousand years, raising the suspicion that a religious attitude has been around a long time.[10] But as any historian will tell you, even with texts, issues of interpretation and context are still challenging.

Our originality as knowers puts us in a very odd position as a species. We are so adept at reading invisible intents that we are lost without them. We rely upon the invisible to make sense of the visible, to make sense of life. Our minds do not sit easily with not knowing; given a blank slate, we will see intents. We make theories, tell stories, find purpose and, in short, fill in the blanks. This includes the blank slate of the past; this includes the blank slate of the cosmos. The odd thing is that we can be wrong—and at some level we know that too.

Nonetheless, over time, our knack for reading minds and sensing invisible causes has helped us as a species to understand the world in ever deeper ways—whether a smile, a gesture, the migration seasons of antelopes, fire, or the growth patterns of barley. And tangled up with such knowing are the gods—those nonobservable entities, the "more," angels and demons, ghosts and spirits, and the Makers of the world itself. At least for the past few thousand years, religion has been all tangled up in our sense-making, intent-reading ways of knowing, which in turn have opened up an amazing cosmos filled with more invisible powers than we can even imagine.

For this reason, religious knowing could be much older, very old in fact—older than cave paintings and burials or language. It could be older than our species, older than several hominid species. Religious knowing

---

10. As Julian Jaynes points out, in some of our oldest written stories and songs (for example, the *Illiad*, *Epic of Gilgamesh*, *Epic of Tukulti-Ninurta*, or parts of the Bible), we know more about the intentions of the gods than we do the human characters involved. Jaynes, *Origins of Consciousness*, 72.

could be as old as the ability to share intentions, to see intents behind intents and causes behind causes. It may be that the originality of human knowing awakened the possibility for religious knowing in our species, that our ways of knowing put us in a position to believe in "something there," an "unseen order," the gods or God, spirits, ancestors, Makers, divine will, or a combination of these to which we seek to adjust our lives, coordinate our ways of being, and share our intentions with this realm of more.

But I could be wrong. Like burials and cave paintings, we simply don't know. The age of religion may remain a blank slate forever. "The tree of knowledge," writes Abraham Heschel, "grows upon the soil of mystery."[11]

11. Heschel, *Man Not Alone*, 7.

15

Primed for More

WHETHER RELIGION IS OLDER than the species or not, the sheer presence and prevalence of religions, religious practices, rituals, beliefs, attitudes, and institutions—and for so long—raises the question: Why? Why does religion persist? Why, generation after generation, do people believe in gods and goddesses, one God, spirits, a Creator, guardian angels, demons, or other invisible beings that engage our lives? Why do people believe in and even orient their lives to unseen orders, and do so consistently all around the world, in nearly every culture?

Even the exceptions—such as atheism or agnosticism—seem to prove the rule. Thoroughgoing atheism is historically new, relatively rare, and often arises in protest to one particular aspect of religious belief (such as an afterlife, divine omnipotence, reincarnation, or creationism) that many religious practitioners don't necessarily buy into either. In short, as Pascal Boyer asks, "Why do people have religion, more or less everywhere?"[1]

Religious Education?

One answer could be religious education.

I have already suggested that the peculiarly human ability not only to read intentions, but share them, might be involved in the origins of religious knowing. The originality of human knowing, chapter 13 observed, makes sharing knowledge and education possible. This includes religious beliefs and practices. These too can be shared among people and passed along from one generation to another. Religious education—intentionally

1. Boyer, *Religion Explained*, 48.

teaching others, particularly children, the beliefs, authorities, knowledge, wisdom, ways, and practices of a religious community—is certainly an important manner by which religious attitudes are sustained and flourish generation after generation. The meme-like, self-sustaining quality of beliefs and practices could account for at least some of religion's ubiquity.

In fact, few from within religion or from without would disagree. Our original knowing not only makes education possible, but religious education. And once—whether one million years ago or five thousand—some of our ancestors told their children about the animal spirits or God or an invisible world, the ideas then rooted, spread, and took on a life of their own.

But there is another school of thought that is not so sure that religious education—whether in the form of intentional teaching or religious socialization—really captures the whole story. Just because we pass along knowledge of religious matters from one generation to another does not mean that we wouldn't sense "more" or wonder about an unseen order or sense nonobservable agencies anyway. There is little doubt that religious education gives particular form to religious knowing, but it could do so and still not be its origin any more than English is the source of my capacity for language. The question for many scholars (like Boyer) who approach religion from the perspective of cognitive science is whether or not our minds predispose us toward a religious attitude. Are we cognitively primed to know the "more"? In a manner analogous to the way a baby's attention is drawn to faces and smiles, are human beings fundamentally drawn toward a spiritual world around them?

Cognitive psychologist Justin Barrett has been particularly thoughtful and articulate about these matters. In his book *Why Would Anyone Believe in God?* Barrett explores the "natural foundations of religion," and in doing so shows the possible link between the cognitive abilities of humanity (including reading intentions) and religious knowing.[2] He contends "that people commonly believe in gods because of the way our minds work in the sorts of natural and social environments we inhabit. We believe most of what we do—including what we believe exists in the world—because of the operation of numerous mental tools, operating mostly below conscious awareness."[3] These mental tools (which Barrett more carefully inventories and describes in the book) allow us, for example, to detect faces in our environment before we ever understand the word "face" or any word at

[handwritten margin note: neurologically?]

2. In addition see Barrett, "Natural Foundations of Religion."
3. Barrett, *Why?*, 107.

143

In fact many of these mental tools we likely share with our primate ᵤusins—the ability to differentiate animate from inanimate objects, for example, or the ability to read simple intentions. These mental tools work together to help us engage our world without having to reflect on whether a rock is alive or whether this person has a mind or that animal is actually an artifact.[4] Such abilities work in largely non-conscious, unreflective ways, so even a young child can read your mind, interpret your gesture, or know that you have a mind without thinking about it any more than a monarch butterfly has to think about how to migrate.

But how does this relate to religion?

Hypersensitivity

In relation to religious beliefs, at the top of Barrett's list of mental tools is agency detection. As he puts it, we have a particularly sensitive *agency detection device* (ADD). We easily and unconsciously recognize agency in our world, that is, "beings (such as people or animals) that not merely respond to their environment but also initiate action on the basis of their own internal states and desires."[5] The ADD, as Barrett describes it, is the mental ability to determine "whether an object is an agent or whether some event or trace is the result of agency."[6]

We live in a world teeming with agents, that is, with creatures that initiate action and leave traces of their actions all around us. And we are good at—even made to—notice them. Doing so may have kept our evolutionary ancestors on the alert for predators—the snap of a twig, the rustling of leaves, a flash of movement in the corner of an eye might signal a lion or tiger or bear, oh my! Better to presume agency first (a dangerous agent at that) and be proven wrong than the other way around.[7] The more ambiguous the information (say an unexpected noise in the dark), the more the reason to presume something's out there.

Humans are so geared toward detecting agency, suggests Barrett, that we sometimes imbue agency where it does not actually exist—in my car that refuses to start, in the stairway that tripped me, or in a bowling pin that doesn't want to fall. In effect, the ADD is hypersensitive, and therefore

4. See ibid., ch. 1
5. Ibid., 4.
6. Ibid., 125.
7. Ibid., 31.

144

Barrett playfully calls it the HADD, our *hypersensitive agency detective device*. "Given HADD's eagerness to identify things as agents, and to find agency around us," says Barrett, "it is no wonder that we yell at our cars and computers, assume that the creaking of a settling house is caused by intruders, and easily understand colors and lines on film as actual characters with a rich mental life—a life for which we have no direct evidence."[8]

blaming
G →

In all, according to this cognitive angle on religion, our minds are primed to sense agency everywhere, and we do so with the slightest sign of life, and sometimes even without it. The human mind is ready to sense agency in the things we see in the light of day, but also in the dark, in things unseen. We are primed to know "something there."

primed?

Theory of Mind

To top matters off, wherever humans sense agency they also sense minds. In philosophical and psychological terms, we each operate with the assumption that others have minds (intents, motivations, emotions, desires, knowledge, beliefs, and more) just as we know ourselves to have minds. We operate with a theory of mind. What may begin as some fairly simple reading and sharing of intentions in the first year of life, becomes more and more complex through early childhood. By the time most children are five years old they not only understand that other people have intents and desires, but they understand that others have very specific kinds of knowledge, perspectives, or beliefs about the world that differ from those of their own.

A good example of this is in the test for so-called false belief. A typical test for false belief that developmental and cognitive psychologists have devised, and I have performed myself,[9] goes something like this: I show a three-year-old, Juan, a box of crayons and ask him, "What do you think is in the box?" Juan responds, "Colors." I open the box and pour out the contents—it's rocks. He's surprised. I now ask Juan, "If I showed this box to your best friend, Jill, and it's the first time Jill has seen the box, what will she think is in the box?" Juan says, "Rocks."

Juan—if he's typical of most three- and four-year-olds—answers "Rocks" even though he knows he himself had been fooled.[10] Juan does

8. Ibid., 40.

9. See Wigger, "See-Through Knowing," and Wigger et al., "Invisible Friends."

10. There is a rich history of these types of tasks that are rooted in the work of Jean

a theory of mind, that is, he understands that others have thoughts and beliefs, but he does not yet differentiate what he himself knows from what others know (whether a friend, parent, or even a dog). He does not yet understand that others can be deceived and could have a false belief about the box. But do the test again when he is five or six years old, Juan will likely answer, "Colors. My friend Jill will be fooled and think there are colors in the box." By this age, most children understand that others can have false beliefs, and that others have points of view and knowledge that may be different from their own. More and more then, as children grow, they begin to appreciate not only that others have knowledge different from their own, but that such knowledge—or wisdom—could be helpful or valuable or worth having too, whether coming from a friend, parent, or teacher. The relevance for religious knowing is that whenever we sense agency, our minds sense another mind, a being that has intentions and desires and motivations and knowledge. Hypersensitive agency detection combined with a theory of mind would seem to be the right kind of cognitive soil for sensing so-called supernatural agents, nonobservable entities, or even an ultimate unseen agent, a Creator behind all agency whose purposes, intentions, and wisdom are at work in creation. And with our ability to share intentions, we may find ourselves trying to share in the intentions behind all intentions.

Divine Wisdom

To explore further the relationship between theory of mind development and religious ideas, Justin Barrett put an inspired twist on the false belief tests: he asked children about God. In a study among children raised in Protestant homes (so believing in one God) he showed them a box of crackers that turned out to have rocks inside. His results replicated other such studies—virtually all three-year-olds and most four-year-olds said that their mothers (as well as other entities, such as a bear and a tree) would know that rocks were in the box. Most five-year-olds and virtually all

---

Piaget's perspective-taking challenges among children. See Piaget and Inhelder, *Child's Conception of Space*. For a good summary of the next wave of research into theory of mind see Moses and Chandler, "Review." For an analysis of cross-cultural findings see Wellman et al., "Meta-Analysis." And for a cross-species analysis see Call and Tomasello, "Nonverbal False Belief Task."

six-year-olds said their mothers (and other creatures) would be fooled and think that crackers were in the box.[11]

But Barrett also asked all the children what God would say is in the cracker box. It would be no surprise to learn that three- and four-year-olds answered "Rocks" for God just as they said their mothers and bears would. The interesting result comes with the five- and six-year-olds, who realized that their mothers (and other creatures) would be fooled by the box. When they answered the question, "What will God think is in the box?" they answered, "Rocks." In other words, the five- and six-year-olds believed that God knows the truth even though people will be fooled by appearances. Barrett and some colleagues ran a similar study with Yukatek Mayan children in Quintana Roo, Mexico, and got similar results. Among the older children, the Catholic God would know what's in the box, and the Sun (part of the Mayan pantheon) and forest spirits were more likely to know than people, but less likely to know than God.[12]

In summary, these children were able to differentiate what other people know from what they themselves know. But they could also differentiate what other people know from what God (or the Sun or forest spirits) would know. In other words, these children could imagine a point of view that cannot be fooled, a source of knowledge that knows what's really inside a box, and they could do so at a young age. Barrett and others who take a cognitive approach to religion argue that this ability to differentiate what God and spirits know from what parents and people generally know is evidence that the gods are not simply people or parents projected onto the universe. Otherwise more five-year-olds would also project limited knowledge onto God when they understand that people—even parents—have limited knowledge and a finite perspective.[13]

In addition, having super-knowledge makes such beings very valuable to human beings. In the case of God, as Barrett points out, "Whether I am concerned about the weather, the harvest, whether my neighbor is stealing from me, the behavior of my children, or the actions of faraway

---

11. Barrett et al., "God's Beliefs." See also Barrett et al., "When Seeing Is Not Believing."

12. See Knight et al., "Children's Attributions," and Knight, "Yukatek Mayan." In addition, I am currently involved in similar cross-cultural research. See Wigger, "Phase II" for updates on the research.

13. For more on this, see Barrett and Richert, "Anthropomorphism"; and Wigger, "See-Through Knowing." Even if children have been taught that God knows everything, the striking fact is that the teaching takes hold so easily (when plenty of other lessons do not).

government officials, God knows and may be concerned and involved." In other words, this makes religion profoundly relevant to people's lives in small and big matters alike, a source of insight and wisdom for living, not simply a matter of an afterlife or eternal destiny. If God knows what's really inside the box, knows all there is to know, imagine how valuable it would be to share in even the tiniest fraction of that knowledge. Guidance, truth, insight, direction—in short, wisdom—would flow.

Likewise, those who appear to have access to this wisdom would also be important sources of guidance and direction—from gurus, ministers, and monks to Sunday school teachers, shamans, and television evangelists. The human mind is drawn to those who may know what's inside the box, who can fill in the blanks—those who seem to know what's really going on in the universe (whether they actually know or not).

Eternally Lost or Explained Away?

Does hypersensitivity to agency explain away religion? Some think so. For example, Richard Dawkins uses Barrett's description of HADD to help make his case for atheism in *The God Delusion*.[14] Religion is simply a by-product of a mind that too easily senses agency and does so even where there is none. The gods are nothing but a projection of mind reading gone crazy against the blank slate of the universe.

This could be true.

Then again, in an interview with the *New York Times* called "Darwin's God," Justin Barrett, himself a practicing Christian, commented on the issue. "Suppose science produces a convincing account for why I think my wife loves me—should I then stop believing that she does?" He points out that "Christian theology teaches that people were crafted by God to be in a loving relationship with him and other people. Why wouldn't God, then, design us in such a way as to find belief in divinity quite natural?"[15]

Whether one believes that the gods or God or spirits or an unseen order or invisible agencies are real—in the sense that they exist apart from

---

14. See Dawkins, *God Delusion*, 184ff. Rather than a byproduct, another school of thought suggests that religion emerged when a whole host of traits, mental tools, behaviors, practices, and abilities combined and became something new, transforming the constituent parts. For a good summary of the issue, see Sosis, "Adaptationist-Byproduct Debate."

15. Henig, "Darwin's God."

our beliefs in them—is every bit as tricky as interpreting burials and paintings. We are dealing in realities and hidden intents that are irreducible to the senses, and therefore they are never entirely accessible to empirical observation or testing. They cannot be proven on scientific grounds any more than the intents of our prehistoric ancestors can be proven when they buried their dead or left handprints on a cave wall.[16] But they cannot be disproven either. And this is a humbling realization for religious and skeptic alike.

A scientific, empirical approach to knowing is powerful in many ways, helping us to better understand who we are and how our minds work. It is a kind of third-person perspective that searches for common ground by stepping outside the particular perspective of any one religion or person's experience of it. Our originality as knowers allows us to do so, to transcend an individual perspective and imagine a point of view that knows all (even if I or we do not). That is, while we experience life from "within," so to speak, we can imagine a point of view from "without." But they are not the same and the temptation is to reduce one to the other.

The hidden cost of the scientific approach is that knowing "from within" is ignored or lost. To describe knowing in a general, third-person manner that looks for common ground is accomplished by ignoring the first-person experience—the *within-ness*—of life, for example, what it is like for Justin Barrett to believe his wife loves him. In terms of the religious life, it is to ignore what it feels like to worship, pray, sense holiness, be inspired, gain insight, give alms, offer sacrifices, be awakened, or recognize the sacred in another. The empirical approach brackets the *within-ness* of religious knowing—why these holy things matter to my life and to our shared life together. The bird's-eye view of the forest, by itself, misses life among the trees. By itself such a perspective reduces the "more" to less. It is like cutting off the right hand in Escher's *Drawing Hands*.

Then again, within any particular variety of religious experience there are plenty of ways of doing the same, that is, reducing the "more" to less. I can assume that my experience of the sacred as a Presbyterian Christian is what religion is like for others, or what it should be like, or that it represents the one true way, or that those of other religions or nonbelievers are eternally lost. There are far too many examples—even within my own little

16. Even material signs (like a healing or speaking in tongues) that might confirm the spiritual "hidden order" in a visible way (for the believer) can always be interpreted in alternative ways.

corner of one room of one house of religion—of reducing the fullness of knowing to a first-person (singular or plural) cloister of narrow-mindedness. Life among the trees can get quite nasty without a larger perspective. From within, it is easy to forget the left hand.

Seeing in Depth

Scientific observation and religious belief alike can reduce the "more" to less. But science and religion alike can open our eyes to see in depth, to be attentive to the hidden powers at work animating the world we do see.

I would simply notice, then, that whether or not it was given by the Makers, our originality as knowers allows us to see life and the universe in deep and powerful ways. Our ability to sense agency, to read intents behind intents, to appreciate points of view outside of our own, and to imagine a knowledge that cannot be deceived, when combined, put us in a posture that is open to a sense of *more*. More to the world than meets the eye, more to other people, and even more to ourselves. We can even know that there is more to know than we could ever know.

16

In the Beginning

"IN THE BEGINNING," DECLARES Martin Buber, "is relation."[1] Like the flap of the butterfly's wing, a little mind reading among some hyper-social primates, over time, generates a tornado of meaning, and the world has never been the same. We are creatures who find ourselves facing a universe that is, in the words of the great physicist Freeman Dyson, "infinite in all directions."[2]

Reflecting Reflections

The strangest thing happens when people share intentions—something not so different from stepping into a funhouse of mirrors—and it can make you dizzy.

Whether you and I are taking a walk together or picking blueberries or carrying a log across a field, the ability to share intentions requires that I read your mind and that you read mine. In doing so I have a place in my mind (an idea or representation) for your intentions and you have such a place in your mind for mine. That is just for starters, and it's about as unconscious to us as blinking. But matters get more complicated.

To actually share these intentions I also have to be aware, at some level, of my own intentions in relation to your intentions; you have to be aware of yours in relation to mine as well. It is as if we are holding up mirrors for one another, each of us seeing the other as well as our own reflection and back again, generating an infinite series of reflections.

1. Martin Buber, *I and Thou*, 18.
2. Dyson, *Infinite in All Directions*.

Call it a recursion of intentions.

A sense of the infinite derives not simply from my seeing your reflection—reading your intentions. It comes from seeing you seeing me, from reading your intentions—which include you reading mine, which include my reading yours, and so on. I can step into your shoes but, when I do, I see you stepping into mine stepping in yours and we are like monks ascending and descending an eternal staircase in an Escher drawing. In sharing intentions an infinite cosmos of relationship opens.

The crux of human uniqueness is not that we are inherently superior to other creatures or that we are of a vastly different order. Neither is it, from a theological perspective, that God loves people more than other animals, nor is it the case that the whole process of evolution was leading up to a *Homo sapien* finale to crown creation. The originality of human knowing is that we can conceive infinity at all, that we can think about time and eternity, a beginning of the universe and its end, or even wonder about a time before time, or imagine a point of view that sees and knows all there is to know. Our hyper-sociality generates a whirlwind of knowing, and with it comes the sense of ever more.

Reflecting All in All

Christian theologian Wolfhart Pannenberg, in his own work on anthropology and human uniqueness several years ago, used the term *exocentricity* (in contrast to *egocentricity*) to emphasize the ways in which human beings are fundamentally open and oriented toward that which is beyond themselves. We are made to be in relationship, with others, with the world. For the theologian this means, ultimately, we are made to be in relationship with the Creator of life itself: "the so-called openness of the human being to the world signifies ultimately an openness to what is beyond the world, so that the real meaning of this openness to the world might be better described as an openness to God which alone makes possible a gaze embracing the world."[3] For Pannenberg, this openness, this exocentricity, is even another way of talking about what it means to be made in the image of God. We are made to reflect a world-embracing perspective and orient our lives accordingly.

Looking out into the vast universe, I am taken outside of the point of view behind my two eyes; I see an ultimate *You* looking back—not only at

3. Pannenberg, *Anthropology*, 69.

me, but at you, at each "you," at all of creation. "Every particular *Thou*," says Buber, "is a glimpse through to the eternal."⁴ To be made in the image of God is to be made as a reflection of the Origin of all, which is to reflect all in all. "The aim of relation is relation's own being, that is, contact with the Thou. For through contact with every Thou we are stirred with a breath of the Thou, that is, of eternal life."⁵

The infinite is reflected in the faces of one another, opening eternity.

4. Buber, *I and Thou*, 75.
5. Ibid., 63.

PART V

IRREDUCIBLE

"O, WHAT A WORLD of unseen visions and heard silences this insubstantial country of the mind." So opens Julian Jaynes's opus on consciousness. "What ineffable essences, these touchless and unshowable reveries! And the privacy of it all! A secret theater of speechless monologue and prevenient counsel, an invisible mansion of all moods, musings, and mysteries, an infinite resort of disappointments and discoveries. A whole kingdom where each of us reigns reclusively alone, questioning what we will, commanding what we can. . . . An introcosm that is more myself than anything I can find in a mirror. This consciousness that is myself of selves, that is everything, and yet nothing at all—what is it?"[1]

The final section of this book brings us back around to consider life in these invisible mansions of mystery and the dilemmas they create when it comes to knowing. These homes are strange and loopy and paradoxical and who we are. Oddly enough, our intense sociality breeds an intense individuality. Our deeply relational nature allows us to relate not only to others in deep and complex ways, but to ourselves. Recall Douglas Hofstadter's claim quoted in chapter 1: "The self comes into being at the moment it has the power to reflect itself."[2] We have the capacity to see ourselves from a bird's-eye view—to read the intentions at work in our own desires and behaviors and reflect upon them, to share intentions with our own selves as well as others. Individuality and sociality form their own pair of drawing hands.

But this bird's-eye view, this place for reflecting upon our lives and upon other minds and upon life itself, is not a place at all, but a secret theater, an introcosm. And to appreciate intents behind intents is to be aware

1. Jaynes, *Origins*, 1.
2. Hofstadter, *GEB*, 709.

that each other—every *I* or *thou*—reigns over insubstantial countries never touching the light of day. We can never fully know the minds of others. The best we get are glimpses and inferences—a window here, a doorway there. Call it a *theory of invisible mansions.*

17

The Rivers and Falls of Consciousness

CLOSE TO HOME, ACROSS the river from the city of Louisville, Kentucky, there is an ancient rocky riverbed called the Falls of the Ohio. The waters of the Ohio River tumbled over these rocks for thousands of years, but now they are dammed off and diverted to the side, bypassing the drop-off, making the river easier to navigate and leaving the former river bottom dry. Exposed along the limestone bed are countless fossilized reminders of ancient ages teeming with life.

I visit the Falls often; the river and fossils remind me of home.

A Thought Experiment

Today I am writing at the Falls. Perhaps, through the magic of writing, I can provide a peek into this insubstantial country of thoughts and observations streaming about in my own consciousness. This is as close as I can get to an empirical record of the otherwise unobservable. It's a refresher course in the layers of awareness composing this introcosm of consciousness.

Only moments ago I was thinking about James Audubon, the artist and ornithologist, who sat nearby two centuries ago sketching scores and scores of birds for his books. I picked up my sketch book and tried to imagine looking through Audubon's eyes, trying to see the area with the attention of an artist—to really notice, be conscious of, the birds bathing and fishing, the treed horizon, the glittering river, the fossils in the outcropping of limestone near my feet, the shade and shapes and shadows. Downriver I could see hardly a sign of modern life—maybe not so different from what Audubon saw—except for a few power lines off in the horizon above the snaking river. Upriver, the view would startle the bird man: a downtown cityscape, bridges, a train, and the dam eliminating the waterfall itself, even as today it is letting a lot of water through. I jotted down these observations and more.

Yet, even with notes, I cannot capture it all, but only attend to one detail or another—the water, my thirst on this hot day, the sound of the crickets. Or are they tree frogs? I forget. I think that's a cicada. What a strange and fragile beast attention is. I realize I have a Grateful Dead song playing in my mind and can hear Jerry Garcia's guitar. I think it's been in my head all day.

I now realize that I'm off my notes and writing about my awareness now.

I close my eyes, but keep writing. I can still see the river, but with not as much detail. Now, in my mind, I even see myself beside the water, with my sketchbook. But now I'm walking, with Jane—this is a memory from a few years ago. I remember how obsessed I was that day, about consciousness itself. I kept thinking about a story I had read in which a doctor had a strange experience—a blackout, but nobody realized he was out. "How could that be?" I hear/see myself asking Jane. "This doctor blacks out but doesn't pass out, examines a patient, and when he comes to, he's writing."

"Why are you thinking about that on this beautiful day?" she replied.

Echoing Jane from a few years earlier, I answered, "Too much consciousness," referring to myself, not the doctor who didn't have enough.

When I get home today, I'll have to ask Jane if she remembers that day. I just opened my eyes as I wrote the last sentence.

As I continue to write, I am thinking of my dream. Original knowing—are we conscious when we dream? From the outside, asleep; on the inside, awake? Well no, not exactly. If consciousness is like a light, is it on or off while we dream? Or maybe there's a nightlight of consciousness? Actually, why do I care? Surely we did eat from the tree of knowledge—cursed with knowing about knowing. Knowing—not knowing. How much of today will you even remember, Bradley? More, I suppose, since you're/I'm writing some of it.

How old are these fossils anyway? Devonian I think, but how old is that? I wonder what they knew. Could trilobites have blackouts? What would that even mean? What if I were blacked out now—how would I know? Could I write? Maybe—the doctor examined a patient.

My son David just popped into my mind—when he was five or six years old. I'm remembering how he could add double-digit numbers instantly, without counting toes or carrying tens or even thinking about it. David lost the ability when he learned double-digit addition in school. I can see him in my mind, on the shore of Lake Winnebago in Wisconsin, demonstrating for his grandparents. He has on some crazy yellow and black pants. I remember asking him how he did it and he went into a long, drawn out, nonsensical explanation that could not have been true. He was just making up an answer, but I don't think he thought he was making it up. David could add without being conscious of how he did it. A doctor could examine a patient without being conscious of anything. I'm thirsty.

I was just taken by the sight of a Blue Heron landing on a sandbar. I became absorbed by the glisten of the river nearby. Hundreds, thousands of sunlit reflections bouncing off the surface. Beautiful.

The guitar is in my head again. Or did it ever go away? Just playing in the background while I attend to the stream of consciousness. A river of consciousness. No, the metaphors are all wrong. Okay, enough of this, readers won't like it. I don't think I'll use it.

Reflection

Whether you liked it or not, even in this conscious attempt to provide a glimpse of consciousness, I realize how polymorphous and multilayered this inner universe is and how difficult it is to capture. Internal thoughts, external observations, memories, points of view, dialogues, stories, and more flowing and eddying about in the Ohio River of my mind. Trying to catch thoughts is like trying to catch dreams—most fade rapidly even when trying to write them down. And I'm sure the writing itself skewed my reflections and awareness, knowing someone might read them. Even so, perhaps I was able to provide a taste of the energetic reflections and inner dialogues and existential questions swirling about my mind this day, all invisible to anyone else at the time. From within, it's a bustling even if insubstantial country. From without, a middle-aged man sitting along the Falls of the Ohio.

Dr. Z

Coming home after this thought experiment at the Falls, I did ask Jane whether she remembered the earlier visit to the Falls and the story about the doctor's blackout. She remembered both. We estimated the day to have been some five years previous. The story had come from a book by Adam Zeman with the clever title *Consciousness: A User's Guide*, and this strange experience of the doctor sharpens the stakes when it comes to conscious awareness and why it matters to our life as knowers, even original knowing.[1]

As a neurologist, Zeman regularly works with patients who have various brain disorders that often lead to strange experiences like the doctor had—in his case due to epilepsy—experiences that raise large questions about the nature of conscious awareness itself. Zeman himself had gotten the story elsewhere, from an article in *Brain*, a major journal in the field of neurology. The event itself had happened over a century ago. Dr. Hughlings-Jackson, a groundbreaker in neurological research, wrote about the event in an article published in 1888. But Hughlings-Jackson was not the doctor who had had the blackout; that was another yet, an anonymous "Dr. Z."

So, at the Falls (in 2011), I was remembering talking with Jane (in 2006) about something I had read (in 2003) quoted by Zeman (in 2002), who had gotten it from Hughlings-Jackson (in 1888), who had gotten it from Dr. Z, who had written it down (in late 1887). And though its resemblance to the childhood game of Grapevine, I was able to get a copy of the original article, and again, through the magic of writing, we are able to read the anonymous doctor's own words as if they were written this morning: "I was attending a young patient whom his mother had brought me with some history of lung symptoms," the so-called Dr. Z wrote. "While he was undressing I felt the onset of a petit-mal. I remember taking out my stethoscope and turning away a little to avoid conversation. The next thing I recollect is that I was sitting at a writing table in the same room, speaking to another person, and as my consciousness became more complete, recollected my patient, but saw he was not in the room."[2]

This is the first-hand account of what happened, how he remembers the episode. Yet obviously there is a hole in his experience. Something is missing—the something that normally allows us to directly know our

1. Zeman, *Consiousness*, 122–23.
2. Hughlings-Jackson, "Epilepsy," 206.

experiences, something crucial to knowing and without which we cannot even imagine what life would be like. Though he was there, Dr. Z's consciousness was not.

At this point in the doctor's account, paradoxically, he has to piece together his own first-hand activities in a second-hand way. "I was interested to ascertain what had happened," Dr. Z writes, "and had an opportunity an hour later of seeing him [the patient] in bed, with the note of a diagnosis I had made of 'pneumonia of the left base.' I gathered indirectly from conversation that I had made a physical examination, written these words, and advised him to take to bed at once. I re-examined him with some curiosity, and found that my conscious diagnosis was the same as my unconscious—or perhaps I should say, unremembered—diagnosis had been."[3]

This unremembered exam, while the most dramatic, was only one of several incidents involving "periods of automatism without memory," as the anonymous doctor called them. Most of these events occurred over the period of just a few months. One involved arriving at the steps of a home with the last memory of sitting on a train. Judging by the absence of his ticket, he would have had to have changed trains and walked half a mile to the house. Another instance involved hiking a treacherous stretch of a Swiss glacier with no memory (and no injury). Yet another incident involved losing consciousness while continuing to play tennis. In all these other cases, the doctor carried through with the activity he had set out to do.[4]

It is tempting, and at least partially accurate, to compare these events to the more common experience of realizing you have driven the last three miles of your commute home with no memory of your travel, or that you have read two pages of a book with no idea of what you just read. You go into some sort of automatic mode. However, there is a difference here. While not remembering the drive or the content of the reading, most people can remember what they were thinking about, what they were conscious of. But in the case of the doctor there was a void.

That which was missing in Dr. Z's experience is that aspect of human consciousness that matters so much to us. Consciousness is that part of our knowing lives that is aware of what is happening as it is happening. Antonio Damasio calls it "the feeling of knowing—the feeling of what happens," or as Gerald Edelman puts it, "the remembered present."[5] Consciousness

3. Ibid., 206–7.
4. Ibid., 201–7.
5. Damasio, *Feeling*," 26; Edelman, *Wider*, 4.

in this sense is likely quite old, not unique to our species, and is heavily intertwined with the ability to make memories. Anesthesiology today has found the way to sedate a patient just enough to shut down memory formation even as the person is able to talk and interact with the doctor. For the person who's been anesthetized, as it was for Dr. Z, it's a little freaky.

More narrowly, self-consciousness[6]—the sense of *I*—could be a more recent development; Jaynes believed it to be unique to humans and quite young (more recent than written language).[7] But I suspect that consciousness, even in this more limited sense, is still tied to mind reading and joint attention, that is, the ability to see ourselves as if through the eyes of another. And this ability could be very old, older than the species.

Irreducible

In the end, consciousness is more than one thing, more than the metaphor of a light would suggest—to be either switched on or off. It is more than a stream or river or country or theater or mansion. Conscious awareness engages a whole host of physical and mental systems, from memory and reflection to attention and the senses. Disruptions in any of these can easily disturb consciousness or, as in the case of Dr. Z, even how we ordinarily think about consciousness.

For all these reasons and because of this complexity, a person's consciousness is irreducibly unique. Like Dr. Z, you or I could have a blackout, but you or I could never have Dr. Z's blackout. Like I did, you could sit along the Falls of the Ohio, see the same river, feel the same sun beating down, sit at the same table, get thirsty, even think about thinking while doing so—but you could never do so exactly as I did that day, let alone have all the same thoughts and questions and reflections. In fact, I could not even do it. At best I can remember my own experience and try to repeat it, but it will never be the same.

So, in this sense, perhaps it is fair to say that each person's conscious experience can be called *original knowing*, that is, unique to each person. We can share intentions within ourselves, create an interpretive matrix among the inner crowd of remembered people and events, even among our

---

6. What Damasio calls "the autobiographical self" (*Feeling*, 199) and Edelman calls "higher-order consciousness" (*Wider*, 97).

7. Jaynes, *Origins*, ch. 3.

remembered selves—the *I* when I was five or 35, or the *I* of a few moments ago who promised himself to quit working by six o'clock today.

In addition, not only is each person's conscious experience original, each moment of consciousness is an original, passing quickly and only accessible again through memory or writing or (like Dr. Z) through the account of others. As every minute ticks away, even each second, we are banned from the garden of experience in which we have just been dwelling, and we can never return. Yet with each moment comes something new, another original.

Still, the fruit of this originality comes with a price, with complications—a mess of questions and philosophical puzzles concerning what matters and what is real and what role our knowing plays in the course of things, if anything at all.

18

Stranger Perspectives

"THIS BOOK IS MY 50th-birthday present to myself," writes Kurt Vonnegut in his novel *Breakfast of Champions*. "I feel as though I am crossing the spine of a roof—having ascended one slope."[1] By saying this from within the novel itself, the self-referencing words "This book" signal something different from an ordinary work of fiction, told neither from a third-person omniscient point of view nor through the first-person account of a fictional character. Or is it both? Either way, Vonnegut twists the ordinary narrative conventions and we know we are reading a strange loop of a story. And the loop gets stranger.

The book goes along fine describing the adventures of Kilgore Trout (with Vonnegut's voice entering and commenting along the way) but then, about two-thirds of the way in, Vonnegut—the author—shows up in the novel itself, at a cocktail lounge, but does not want to be seen: "I had come to the Arts Festival incognito. I was there to watch a confrontation between two human beings I had created: Dwayne Hoover and Kilgore Trout. I was not eager to be recognized. The waitress lit the hurricane lamp on my table. I pinched out the flame with my fingers."[2]

Vonnegut is both narrator (from the outside) and a character narrating the story (from the inside, at a fictional bar). And by entering his own fictional story and violating ordinary storytelling, Vonnegut makes us more conscious of first- and third-person perspectives, the view from within and without, and performs in writing what Escher could do in drawing.

1. Vonnegut, *Breakfast*, 4.
2. Ibid., 197.

b/c have to use the j. organ trying to explain -> your eyes is you can eye more than w/ your see w/ your

The Dilemma

One of the most fundamental dilemmas in trying to study or understand consciousness can be traced to a basic question: How does the *view from within* relate to the *view from without*? How does the *subjective world* or *first-person perspective* relate to the *objective world* or *third-person perspective* that we use when we study something? Philosopher David Chalmers has dubbed this the "hard" problem of consciousness.[3] How do subjective experiences of the mind relate to objectively observable processes of the brain? While Escher and Vonnegut play with perspectives, the hard problem rears its head among the most serious of scientists who are trying to study the brain itself. In some ways, the more seriously the hard problem is taken, the worse it gets.

For example, when medical researchers study our brains—the actual organ in our skulls—they are examining the perceivable, sensible, empirical world, taking the perspective from without. They are trying to understand and describe how brains function, working from a point of view that can be shared and verified by others. This is how serious science works, thriving on knowledge that is public in nature, and it has led to all kinds of knowledge, including the understanding that brains are involved in the ways we know and experience the world. In contrast to the individual, unique, private theater experience of one's mind, science, as Adam Zeman puts it, involves "a meticulous effort to eliminate subjectivity, to achieve a reproducible, 'impersonal' description of the world, an account on which all disinterested observers can agree."[4] Scientific description is based upon points of view that can be shared.

But in practice, matters are not so clean-cut. A neurologist like Zeman, for example, must rely upon both points of view, from within and from without, subjective and objective. First of all, it is usually the disruption of the first-hand view from within that leads a patient to the doctor—a blackout, pain, or memory loss for example. And these first-hand experiences provide crucial information about what is going on in the scientifically understood brain and vice versa. A blackout could be a sign of epilepsy in the brain. The plaques and tangles of an Alzheimer's-diseased brain could be the reason for memory loss. Food allergies or emotional stress could trigger the first-person pain of a migraine. Both kinds of information—a patient's

3. Chalmers, *Conscious Mind*, xiii.
4. Zeman, *Consciousness*, 5.

experience and scientific knowledge—are crucial for the field of medicine, if not the field of life. But they are different kinds of knowledge flowing out of two very different points of view. "First person accounts evoke a single point of view, while scientific accounts abstract features of the world common to all points of view."[5] One is unique to each person and invisible to others while the other is common and visible to potentially anyone.

Researchers could wire up my brain in a sleep lab, and they could tell you when I am dreaming and for how long, and they could tell what parts of the brain appear to be most active during the dream. They could tell you how the neurons in my brain work, how the dendrites and axons of brain cells communicate with one another at synapses, how synapses themselves are chemical reactions; and they could tell you much, much more. But, for all this information, the researchers could not tell you what I dreamed—the specific images and words, sounds, or smells I experienced while dreaming. They could not tell you I dreamed that I wrote a book called *Original Knowing*, let alone what it felt like to have such a dream, or what I think the dream means, if anything.

If others had been with me at the Falls of the Ohio, they too could have seen the blue heron, or studied the fossils, or felt the heat of the sun. Unlike my thoughts, anyone with working eyes could have seen the blue heron. While we might have argued about whether it was a blue heron or an egret, in principle, the debate could have been settled with more observation. In fact even the notion of "in principle" relies upon an imagined third-person, shared perspective to which the truth of the situation conforms. Scientific description is the basis for understanding how the world we share works, including our brains. It relies upon direct observations and leads to theories deduced from those observations. But, for all this information about the landscape and fauna at the Falls, nobody could have told you what was going on in the mindscape of my thoughts (without reading my account)— the reveries, the reflections, or the connections to dreams and books and memories from years before.

So when it comes to scientifically studying the human mind, we get all tripped up in the tangled loops of perspectives. We are trying to shine a public light on that which is invisible. The best we can do is describe that first-person experience to others, but inevitably something is lost in translation. Our representations of reality—our maps—are never the same as the original.

5. Ibid.

So, secret theater or public stage? The sheer presence of both realms of knowing stirs the questions considered for millennia by thoughtful people. *Mind-body dualism, subject-object split,* and *idealism verses materialism* are but a few shorthand ways of referring to the basic dilemma. How do publicly visible bodies give rise to private invisible thoughts and feelings or how do subjective thoughts lead to objective actions?

Doubt and Suspicions

However named, the temptation is to cast doubt on the validity of one realm of knowing or the other. Maybe consciousness is not only elusive, but an illusion. Or maybe the publically shared world observed through the senses is itself a deception.

In Plato's *Republic*, for example, Socrates describes a cave in which prisoners have been chained to chairs all their lives facing a wall. A fire behind them creates shadows on that wall. "To them," says Socrates, "the truth would be literally nothing but the shadows of the images."[6] Plato uses this analogy to argue that the world of sight, the physical world known by our senses, is inherently naïve—our senses mistake the dark, fleeting, two-dimensional shadows for the real thing. The prisoners have to be unchained and released to be able to recognize their error. Entering the sunlit world outside the cave, though initially blinded by the light, they will eventually see the truth.

Strangely enough, for Plato, going outside the cave takes you inside the mind. For him, the path of enlightenment is a journey away from the temporal, dying body and its senses and toward the eternal life of Ideas accessed through education and contemplation. There is a world of perfect, unchanging Forms—the ultimate in knowing—beyond the everyday forms we see with our deceiving eyes. In this case, *original knowing* through our senses is actually an *original deception*—that is, if Plato is right.

Some two thousand years after Plato, Rene Descartes took the suspicion of our senses and bodies a step further, by wondering whether it's all a dream. In general, he says, he has no reason to doubt that "I am here, seated by the fire, wearing a winter dressing gown, holding this paper in my hands . . . ." Only a troubled brain would doubt or "deny that these hands and this body are mine." But then again, "How many times has it occurred that the quiet of the night made me dream of my usual habits: that I was

6. Plato, *Republic*, 254.

here, clothed in a dressing gown, and sitting by the fire, although I was in fact lying undressed in bed!"[7]

Because we are aware that our dreams can trick us so easily, perhaps we are really asleep even when we are so sure we are awake and know the difference. Our eyes, heads, and bodies themselves could be illusions. Descartes is able to raise doubts about everything he can think of except one thing—his own thinking. "I could imagine that I had no body, and there was no world nor any place that I occupied, but that I could not imagine for a moment that I did not exist."[8] From this Descartes concluded that this *I* (also called *ego, soul, mind*) was a "substance whose whole essence or nature was only to think" needing no space or body, and in fact even without the body, "the soul would not cease to be all that it now is."[9]

Notice what the great thinker has done in relation to the inside-outside perspective. When Descartes raises the possibility that we could be dreaming even when we are awake, he is raising the possibility that there is no outside, objective world or view from without—it's all inside our minds. Life as we know it could be but a dream, shadows on a cave wall. The only thing I cannot doubt is that I can think about this, and because I can think, therefore I am.

Out of this tradition has come a great emphasis upon thought, ideas, theory, and reason when it comes to what matters in knowing, in what is true. Along with it has come an emphasis upon mathematics and logic because, as Descartes says, whether awake or asleep, "two and three together will always make the number five, and the square will never have more than four sides."[10] In other words, because these facts are unchanging and true to any world, they become the basis of knowledge we can rely upon to cut through the delusions our sensing bodies throw at us. It does not matter that no perfect square actually exists in the world that we sense, however close an object like the top of a box may come. The idea of a perfect square does exist and the truth of it never changes.

Of course, Descartes did not bother to ask his dream question when it came to two plus three or boxes or his own thinking. In other words, using the same method of doubt and suspicion regarding the world sensed and our bodies that sense it, we could also cast doubt and suspicion upon

7. Descartes, *Meditations*, 76.
8. Ibid., 25.
9. Ibid.
10. Ibid., 78.

the thinking mind, the *I*, or the very soul casting doubt. We could d
consciousness itself. Maybe Plato and Descartes had it exactly backwards.
Perhaps it is the case that the self-aware *I*, the feeling of what happens, the
view from within, the subjective world, is itself more like the shadows on a
cave wall. Could it be that the seat of waking awareness and decision making is more like a useful fiction, an illusion? Some are suggesting this route
through the hard problem.

Delays in Time

A big wrinkle in consciousness studies occurred in 1982, when Benjamin
Libet published the results of his neurological experiments concerning the
correlation between consciousness and brain/nerve activity. His conclusion
was that there is nearly a half-second delay between our conscious decision
to do something (like raise a hand), and the brain's neurological activity
that leads to the action. That is, there appears to be a half-second gap between the conscious decision to act and the brain activity leading to the act.
And a half-second is practically an eternity in neurology.

But so what? A half-second does seem a little slower than most of us
would guess. It feels more like I decide to raise my hand and it happens immediately—hardly an illusion worth worrying about. The "so what" is this:
the decision to raise my hand, according to Libet's research, occurs after the
brain has already initiated the action.[11] After! My body raises a hand, then
I "decide" to do so.

The implication is that the body, the brain, the nerve cells in the brain,
initiate actions and then, oh by the way, it only seems like I decided this.
Decisions, in this scenario, are literally afterthoughts, but we don't know
it. Consciousness is a "user's illusion."[12] Our bodies unconsciously interact
with and respond to the world around us—but consciousness rearranges
our awareness and our sense of time so that it feels as if we are the authors of
our actions, if not our lives. And the reordering of time and consequences
also happens unconsciously, that is, without our awareness.

Obviously, if this is true, the implications are radical. Most of us—
philosophers included—believe that consciousness means we are indeed
able to make choices for ourselves, that we are subjects with some degree of

11. Libet et al., "Time."
12. Nørretranders, *User Illusion*.

freedom to make decisions and direct our own lives in so many ways. And here, with Libet's research, such an assumption is up for grabs.

But before you lose your own mind over this, or conclude that Libet has lost his, there are some important loopholes in the conclusion, ones that keep hope alive that individual autonomy, freedom, and will are not impossible, even scientifically considered. The most important factor is the "veto." By Libet's own measures, even though we do not initiate action by conscious will, we can stop an act. As Tor Nørretranders explains in his book on consciousness, "Consciousness cannot initiate an action, but it can decide that it should not be carried out."[13] But if that is true, is there a consciousness within consciousness? Just what does it mean to "decide" to stop an action? Who or what exercises the veto? Whatever the stopping mechanism is, some decision-making *I* seems implicated.[14]

Getting Real

Secret theater or public stage? Are both realms equally real? Can an idea or a dream or a memory be of the same order of reality as a boulder or stethoscope or river? If so, in what sense—the neurons firing in the brain? Or does our understanding of what is real actually shift from one point of view to the other?

From the point of view of the empirical stage, the sensing body knows so much more than our conscious minds ever could. Consciousness is the tip of the knowing iceberg: by some estimates, using some very sophisticated accounting, our conscious awareness works at a rate of somewhere between one and 16 bits of information per second. By the same measure, our bodies normally sense around 11 million bits of information per second. In general then, the ratio between what our bodies sense and what we are consciously aware of is about a million to one.[15]

So perhaps the most original knowing of all, the most basic and fundamental type of knowledge available to us, is the world sensed, that "direct and primitive contact with the world," as philosopher of perception Maurice

13. Ibid., 243.

14. Even one small decision not to do something could easily generate its own butterfly effect over time. For a new study raising questions about Libet's interpretation of his own findings, see Trevena and Miller, "Brain."

15. For a good description of how these figures are calculated see Nørrentranders, *User Illusion*, chs. 6–7.

Merleau-Ponty puts it, a world "already there before reflection begins," a reality known by our bodies beneath whatever we can think or remember or reflect upon.[16] Then again, dreams and ideas and memories that occur in a flash, using only a handful of mental bandwidth at their inception, may endure for a lifetime—or more—such as Plato's cave analogy. How do you measure that? Some philosophical puzzles may endure for millennia.

∞

I have taken a brief foray into each side of the hard problem of consciousness only to provide a taste of the difficulties involved, and to show how strong the temptation has been to solve the problem by casting doubt upon one view or the other. From without, the world of within is the stranger. From within, we can even doubt away the world without. As Adam Zeman concludes at the end of his own book on the subject, "our experience [from within] is marvelously rich *and* utterly dependent on the brain [from without]. Any account of the nature of consciousness must do justice to these facts . . . ."[17] The answer to the hard problem of consciousness will have to find its way along the strange loop between the *half-second delay* and *I think therefore I am*, somewhere between 11 million bits per second of sensory information and the invisible mansion.

The Tree of Knowledge

In light of this book's larger exploration into the deep history of human knowing, we can notice how the hard problem of consciousness has its roots in the kind of mind that can reflect upon its own existence in the world. What may have begun as some extra-social primates reading intentions and sharing them, has led us to a Pandora's box of philosophical conundrums. Eating from the tree of knowledge, we see ourselves from without even as we know ourselves from within. Our reflective, representational abilities are themselves made possible by our ability to read and share intentions. Without the ability to read intents behind intents—to understand as if from another's perspective—there would be no view from without, no point of view that shares all points of view, no third-person

16. Merleau-Ponty, *Perception*, vii.
17. Zeman, *Consciousness*, 341.

perspective, no omniscient standpoint, no angle as if from the gods. Without this view, there would be no ability to detect invisible agents, no ability to scientifically see or describe anything.

This same view allows us to describe the world around us, and within us. But the moment we talk about anything, even the view from within, we are in shared space, an interpretive matrix. In this shared space more and more complex forms of communication have emerged in our species—gesture, sign, symbol, semantics, recursion and more. Our movements and words, our mathematical formulae and sculptures, our dances and music become meaningful to one another as we share in these worlds together. But in so doing, in being immersed in rich cultures of shared knowledge, we develop complex interior worlds, including a self-aware *I* who dwells simultaneously in an invisible mansion and a visible, sensing body.

In a way, our very descriptions play the role of a trickster when it comes to the hard problem. Language and other forms of representation bridge the world without and the world within, as well as bridge distant times and places to the present. Through writing, for example, we have been able to hear about a doctor who blacked out over a hundred years ago and about a dream that happened more recently and an afternoon at the Falls of the Ohio and a trilobite that lived half a billion years ago. Words, here, have re-presented these times and places and experiences. Almost.

It is this *almost* quality of representation that generates trouble. Stories, theories, explanations, and more very easily give the impression of a complete understanding. We can use our words to describe the life and behavior of bats but we will never know what it is like to be a bat—to use a famous example by Thomas Nagel.[18] The same is true of trilobites and butterflies and chimps and even the people you know best. Explaining behavior or thoughts or dreams or language or consciousness or religion—from the shared, third-person perspective—simply is not the same as experiencing them from within. Even the best descriptions are second-hand. All our vehicles of explanation—whether words or mathematical theories—are always and forever at least one step removed from first-hand experiences. But language and theories are so good at what they do that we can easily forget their *almost* quality, forget that there is always so much more to reality than the descriptions we use to talk about it. Our descriptions are always a little deceptive, luring us into believing we know more than we do. (Not to mention, we can intentionally deceive, make stuff up, generate lies or

18. See Nagel, "Bat."

pass them along.) We can mistake the words and representations we use for reality for reality itself.

So with the power to represent, to describe, to talk, to reflect, comes temptation. Lured to "be like God," we can indeed see from another, often greater perspective, even a kind of super-perspective. Like the first humans of the Popol Vuh, we can see all, perfectly, or so it seems. This is the temptation. The danger is that we mistake the bigger picture for the complete picture, that our descriptions explain matters away, or that our maps of reality are reality. Original knowing tempts us to eat from the know-it-all tree.

So, in the paradise of knowing, a certain humility is required in order not to be kicked out forever. Science and religion alike know this, teach this, and at their best cultivate such humility. Science does so by submitting knowledge to the public realm where a larger community can consider it. Religion encourages confession and tells warning stories of deception and overreaching. The practice of science, at its best, cultivates an awareness of our incomplete grasp on truth and openness to the strange and wonderful nature of the universe. Religious practice, at its best, cultivates awareness of mystery, that there is ever more, that life is ever deeper.

Humility does not make the hard problem of consciousness go away, or the devilish temptations of the know-it-all tree, but it may be the beginning of wisdom. Then perhaps, first person and third will be no longer strangers.

∞

When Vonnegut shows up in *Breakfast of Champions*, he is successful in hiding from his main character, Kilgore Trout, at first. However, they finally do meet at the end of the story.

> "Mr. Trout," I said from the unlighted interior of the car, "you have nothing to fear. I bring you tidings of great joy."
>
> He was slow to get his breath back, so he wasn't much of a conversationalist at first. "Are—are you—from the—the Arts Festival?" he said. His eyes rolled and rolled.
>
> "I am from the *Everything* Festival," I replied. . . . "Mr. Trout," I said, "I am a novelist, and I created you for use in my books."
>
> "Pardon me?" he said.
>
> "I'm your Creator," I said. "You're in the middle of a book right now—close to the end of it, actually."[19]

19. Vonnegut, *Breakfast*, 298–99.

Part V: Irreducible

Vonnegut then holds out an object, a symbol, for Trout to see—it's an apple.

19

Home

"So where is this site?" my brother John was asking me.

"Up the river, near Kampsville."

"Kampsville?"

"Yep. We stay on the River Road, past Pere Marquette and on up just beyond Hardin." Hardin is where we would go to pick apples when we were kids. Pere Marquette is an Illinois state park named after the 17th-century French Jesuit who, with Louis Jolliet, were the first Europeans to explore the upper Mississippi River. The park sits where the Mississippi and Illinois Rivers meet, and the tradition is that when the explorers were returning back upriver toward the Great Lakes, local Native Americans—the Ilini-wek—told them about a shortcut, what is now called the Illinois River.

"I haven't been up there in a long time," my brother responded, "I'm game."

∞

Once again it was the day after Thanksgiving, and once again I was headed up the Mississippi River Road, north of my hometown, as I had done a couple of years previously. It was a different brother this time—John instead of Steve—and these were different kids in the back seat—John's boys, Adam and Jackson. We were not hunting for trilobites, we were hunting for a world-famous archeological dig not an hour from where we grew up. The site is called Koster.

I would have been nine years old at the time, John would have been four, in the summer of 1968. An archeologist from Northwestern University named Stuart Struever, at the urging of locals, traipsed through a cornfield on the farm of Theodore and Mary Koster.[1] Professor Struever had spent his summers exploring the Southern Illinois region for the previous decade. Long before Marquette and Jolliet ever met up with the Iliniwek, there were generations and generations of people living and traveling along these rivers, from the Cahokia who were building mounds a thousand years ago, to the even more ancient Hopewell peoples who were living here when Jesus was born. The river waters would have offered plenty of fish and mussels, while the woodlands would have provided plenty of fauna, edible grasses, berries, and nuts. And there were springs—one at Koster in fact.

Already an expert in prehistoric ceramics, when Struever saw pieces of pottery in the plowed surface dirt of the Koster farm he immediately recognized them as being made by the Jersey Bluff people who had lived in the area between 800 and 1200 CE. The field lay near a towering ridge of limestone bluffs, and this turns out to be key to preservation.

"We've got to dig this place," Struever said to the man who got him out there in the first place—a friend of the Kosters. "We've got to dig this place to see if there's anything older underneath."[2] Over the centuries, rain and wind have brought soil down to the field below, soil that had once been atop the bluffs. The soil is called *loess*. The loess has the effect of covering up and preserving any potential cultural artifacts left by the people who had once been there. So, with the full cooperation of the Kosters, Struever did begin a dig on their farm, and kept digging for a decade.

∞

"It's amazing to me," my brother said as we were driving up the river, "all this history here, and you never hear about it." The fact is that neither of us had heard about the Koster dig when we were growing up. I had only recently discovered it,[3] read Struever's own book telling its story, and could hardly wait for my next trip home to pay a visit—which was this day.

"Yeah," I replied to John, "I asked Mom if she had heard about it and she said she thinks maybe she heard something about something going on up there—but it was all very vague." But there was another edge to John's

1. The story of the Koster dig is told first-hand by Stuart Struever in Struever and Holton, *Koster*.

2. Ibid., 11.

3. Thanks to Steven Mithen's *After the Ice*, ch. 31.

comment, and another reason he may have been particularly interested in the site. It is the fact that he is married to Kim, a woman of Choctaw descent, from Oklahoma. Thanks to the shameful legacy of the 1818 Edwardsville Treaty and the 1830 Indian Removal Act, about the only people of indigenous heritage anywhere nearby were sitting in the back seat of the car.

"It's wild to think," I added, "that Adam and Jackson's great, great-great—however many 'greats' it takes—grandparents could have been living here."

I think the comment meant something to my brother, more than I had intended. Even though they live in Chicago, and my family in Louisville, the waters here, the bluffs, the woodlands, the cornfields—in short, this place—feels more like home to both of us than anywhere. The thought that it was once home to his children's ancient ancestors millennia before Marquette and Jolliet was a powerful one, and once again I realized that where we come from, whom we come from, matters.

Original Knowing

Original knowing, as explored in this book, means many things. Here I want to include the sense driving this book: original knowing has something to do with the desire to know our origins, to be connected to a source, to a spring, to life. But sometimes those origins are buried beneath many layers of dirt and loess and cultural prejudices that attempt to blot out the memory of those other than "our own," which seems to me as good a candidate as any for *original sin*.

Streuver's team of "arkies," as they were affectionately called by the locals—mostly archeology students from Northwestern—did indeed find something buried below the Jersey Bluff era, or "horizon" as they call each strata of remains. They dug and collected, scraped and brushed, into nearly 40 feet of earth to discover remains from 25 horizons of living. Some of these involved little more than a temporary campsite of a few days, while others showed signs of continuous dwelling for over a hundred years.[4] The earliest horizon dates to approximately 10 thousand years before the present. So for at least 9,800 years indigenous peoples had been traveling, camping, and living along these rivers and bluffs that I too think of as home.

4. Streuver and Holton, *Koster*, 244.

Not only did the team find hearths and charred seeds, there were duck and fish bones, mussel and snail shells, beads and woven fabric, stone tools and clay daubing for homes. They found a tiny copper serpent that is often interpreted as a religious symbol. They found 25 human burials and, to the surprise of many, three dog burial sites, the oldest from 8,500 years ago. It is the oldest dog burial discovered so far in North America.

Amazing—so many layers of living discovered in this one small section of one small cornfield outside of one very small town along the Illinois River. Who knows how much more was going on?

The Koster site, with its reminder of generations and generations of human dwelling, is a reminder to me of just how fragile and full of holes human knowing is. Knowing, it would seem, is always something like a handful of anthropologists or archeologists spread out over a massive planet looking here and there for clues to the lives of our predecessors who could have been about anywhere. There is so much more to know than we can know. Sometimes it's right under your nose and you don't even realize it.

or inside your head

Paradoxically, the Koster site reminds me that we can know a lot. We can take a handful of dirt and pottery, dig into the ground and examine seeds and bones and beads, envision scenarios and deduce behaviors, and then begin to sense the richly lived lives of people thousands of years in the past and recognize our connection to them. Knowing can be complex and multilayered, composed of horizon on top of horizon, and run as deep as an ancient spring.

The Koster dig officially ended in 1979, but that only means that the arkies left the property then. Analysis and interpretation of the artifacts and pollens, the soil and the seeds, continue. The dig itself involved thousands of students over the decade, that is, thousands of young people traipsing and driving in and out of the Koster farm and making a mess—a big, albeit fascinating, hole—but a mess all the same. Theodore and Mary Koster donated the land, and in fact replaced their wearing wooden bridge over the creek with a concrete one to handle the traffic. In addition they cleaned up an old rock pioneer house so the arkies could use it however they needed. As one of them put it, "I think the Kosters are more like American Indians than like other Americans, even if they don't realize it. . . . They don't ever say, 'This land is mine' or do anything to exploit the people who come here. They simply welcome everybody and say, 'Come share it with us.'"[5]

5. Ibid., 72.

The statement reminds me again how the roots of human knowing may well rest in sharing.

∞

After a good bit of searching, my brother and I found the farm. As we drove up I felt a strange mix of anxiety and attraction. Having learned so much about the past of this particular place—thousands of years—from Streuver's book, the site felt sacred, seemed as holy ground, so much so that it was overwhelming and I did not want to disturb any spirits not to mention the family still living there. Like Moses before the burning bush, I wanted to take off my sandals.

Instead we simply stopped the car and stared quietly. Even the kids were silent.

Wonder

Now, a thousand miles from home, I sit in my pew along the lake in Northwestern Ontario and wait for the end of the day. I hope for a glimpse of those magical lights tonight, but the past few have been cloudy and tomorrow I leave. Part of me thinks, "What better way to end my book than with the same glorious vision of the sky with which I began."

"Wonder alone," writes Abraham Heschel "is the compass that may direct us to the pole of meaning."[6]

Whether in science or religion, knowing works best by the power of wonder. Perhaps the greatest challenge for our species—our best shot of being creatures worthy of another couple hundred millennia of life—is to cultivate wonder. Wonder in the face of the universe. Wonder in the face of one another. Wonder in the community of creation. Wonder knows the world is ever bigger than our conscious awareness of it. Wonder knows the view from within is only part of the picture and knows the same for the public view. Wonder inspires the awareness of beauty and mystery, and delights in life whether beholding stars or trilobites or the eyes of a newborn beholding you. Wonder is our return to paradise.

"What better way," I think to myself, "to end this pilgrimage into the land of knowing than with the wonder of the northern lights." And as I wait, more and more stars appear overhead—beautiful. I wait some more

6. Heschel, *Man Is Not Alone*, 16.

for the more spectacular offering on the northern horizon, and wait, and wait. Maybe not.

I slowly realize that it does not matter whether I see *aurora borealis* tonight or not. It is good either way. In this place, in this time, the sacred lives. I am grateful.

Bibliography

Aeschylus. *Prometheus Bound*. Translated by E. H. Plumptre. Vol. VIII, Part 4. Harvard Classics 8/4. New York: Collier, 1909–14. Online: http://www.bartleby.com/8/4/.

Allport, Susan. *A Natural History of Parenting: From Emperor Penguins to Reluctant Ewes, A Naturalist looks at How Parenting Differs in the Animal World and Ours*. New York: Harmony, 1997.

Baron-Cohen, Simon. *Mindblindness: An Essay on Autism and Theory of Mind*. Cambridge, MA: MIT Press, 1995.

Barrett, Justin L. "Exploring the Natural Foundations of Religion." *Trends in Cognitive Sciences* 4 (2000) 29–34.

———. *Why Would Anyone Believe in God?* Walnut Creek, CA: Altamira, 2004.

Barrett, Justin L., and Rebekah A. Richert. "Anthropomorphism or Preparedness?: Exploring Children's God Concepts." *Review of Religious Research* 44 (2003) 300–312.

Barrett, Justin L., et al. "God's Beliefs versus Mother's: The Development of Nonhuman Agent Concepts." *Child Development* 72 (2001) 50–65.

———. "When Seeing Is Not Believing: Children's Understanding of Humans' and Non-Humans' Use of Background Knowledge in Interpreting Visual Displays." *Journal of Cognition and Culture* 3 (2003) 91–108.

Berger, Lee. "Viewpoint: Is It Time to Revise the System of Scientific Naming?" *National Geographic News*, December 4, 2001. Online: http://news.nationalgeographic.com/news/2001/12/1204_hominin_id.html.

Berna, F., et. al. "Microstratigraphic evidence of in situ fire in the Acheulean strata of Wonderwerk Cave, Northern Cape province, South Africa." *Proceedings of the National Academy of Sciences of the United States of America* 109/20 (May 15, 2012). DOI: 10.1073/pnas.1117620109. Online: http://www.pnas.org/content/109/20/E1215.full.

Black, J. A., et al. "A Hymn to Ninkasi." In *The Electronic Text Corpus of Sumerian Literature*, t.4.23.1. 2nd ed. Oxford: Faculty of Oriental Studies, University of Oxford, 2006. Online: http://etcsl.orinst.ox.ac.uk/cgi-bin/etcsl.cgi?text=t.4.23.1#.

Boyer, Pascal. *Religion Explained: The Evolutionary Origins of Religious Thought*. New York: Basic Books, 2001.

Brown, Kathryn. "Animal Magnetism Guides Migration." *Science* 294 (October 12, 2001) 283–84.

Brown, P., et al. "A New Small-Bodied Hominin from the Late Pleistocene of Flores, Indonesia," *Nature* 431 (2004) 1055–61.

Brown, Stephen. "The 'Musilanguage' Model of Human Evolution." In *The Origins of Music*, edited by N. L. Wallin et al., 271–300. Cambridge, MA: MIT Press, 2000.

Bibliography

Buber, Martin. *I and Thou*. Translated by Ronald Gregor Smith. New York: Scribner, 1958.

Call, Josep, and Michael Tomasello. "A Nonverbal False Belief Task: The Performance of Children and Great Apes." *Child Development* 70 (1999) 381–95.

Calvin, William. *A Brief History of the Mind: From Apes to Intellect and Beyond*. Oxford: Oxford University Press, 2005.

Carpenter, M., et al. "Social Cognition, Joint Attention, and Communicative Competence from 9 to 15 Months of Age." *Monographs of the Society of Research in Child Development* 63 (1998) 1–143.

Chalmers, David J. *The Conscious Mind: In Search of a Fundamental Theory*. Oxford: Oxford University Press, 1996.

Coles, Robert. *The Spiritual Life of Children*. Boston: Houghton Mifflin, 1990.

Cutler, Alan. *The Seashell on the Mountaintop: How Nicolaus Steno Solved an Ancient Mystery and Created a Science of the Earth*. New York: Plume, 2003.

Damasio, Antonio. *The Feeling of What Happens: Body and Emotion in the Making of Consciousness*. San Diego, CA: Harcourt Brace, 1999.

Dart, R.A. "*Australopithecus Africanus*: The Man-Ape of South Africa." *Nature* 115 (1925) 195–99.

Darwin, Charles. *The Descent of Man and Selection in Relation to Sex*. 2nd ed. 1874. Reprint, New York: D. Appelton, 1909.

Dawkins, Richard. *The God Delusion*. New York: Houghton Mifflin, 2006.

Descartes, René. *Discourse on Method and Meditations*. Translated by Laurence J. Lafleur. Little Library of Liberal Arts. New York: Liberal Arts Press, 1950.

Dyson, Freeman J. *Infinite in All Directions: Gifford Lectures Given at Aberdeen, Scotland, April–November 1985*. New York: Harper & Row, 1988.

Edelman, Gerald M. *Wider than the Sky: The Phenomenal Gift of Consciousness*. New Haven, CT: Yale University Press, 2004.

Eiseley, Loren. *The Immense Journey: An Imaginative Naturalist Explores the Mysteries of Man and Nature*. New York: Vintage, 1957.

———. *The Star Thrower*. New York: Harcourt, 1978.

Erikson, Erik H. *Childhood and Society*. 1950. Reprint, New York: Norton, 1985.

Etheredge, Jason A., et al. "Monarch Butterflies (*Danaus Plexippus* L.) Use a Magnetic Compass for Navigation." *Proceedings of the National Academy of Sciences* 99 (November 23, 1999) 13845–46.

Everett, Daniel. "Cultural Constraints on Grammar and Cognition In Pirahã: Another Look at the Design Features of Human Language." *Current Anthropology* 46 (2005) 621–46.

Gardner, Howard. *Frames of Mind: The Theory of Multiple Intelligences*. New York: Basic Books, 1983.

———. *Intelligence Reframed: Multiple Intelligences for the 21st Century*. New York: Basic Books, 1999.

Gazzaniga, Michael. *Human: The Science behind What Makes Us Unique*. New York: HarperCollins, 2008.

Gibson, Eleanor J. *Principles of Perceptual Learning and Development*. New York: Appleton-Century-Crofts, 1969.

Gibson, James J. *The Ecological Approach to Perception*. Boston: Houghton Mifflin, 1979.

Gleick, James. *Chaos: Making a New Science*. New York: Viking, 1987.

Goodall, Jane. *The Chimpanzees of Gombe: Patterns of Behavior*. Cambridge, MA: Harvard University Press, 1986.

Goren-Inbar, Naama, et al. "Evidence of Hominin Control of Fire at Gesher Benot Ya'aqov, Israel." *Science*, n.s., 304 (April 30, 2004) 725–27.

Greenspan, Stanley I., and Stuart G. Shanker. *The First Idea: How Symbols, Language, and Intelligence Evolved from Our Primate Ancestors to Modern Humans*. Cambridge, MA: Da Capo, 2004.

Groleau, Rick. "When Our Magnetic Field Flips." NOVA website, November, 18, 2003. Online: http://www.pbs.org/wgbh/nova/magnetic/reversals.html.

Hart, Mickey. *Drumming at the Edge of Magic: A Journey into the Spirit of Percussion*. San Francisco: HarperSanFrancisco, 1990.

Hauser, Marc D. "The Faculty of Language: What Is It, Who Has It, and How Did It Evolve." *Science* 298 (November 22, 2002) 1569–79.

Henig, Robin Marantz. "Darwin's God." *New York Times*, March 4, 2007. Online: http://www.nytimes.com/2007/03/04/magazine/04evolution.t.html.

Heschel, Abraham Joshua. *Man Is Not Alone: A Philosophy of Religion*. New York: Farrar, Straus & Young, 1951.

———. *The Sabbath: Its Meaning for Modern Man*. New York: Farrar, Straus, & Young, 1951.

Hofstadter, Douglas R. *Gödel, Escher, Bach: An Eternal Golden Braid: A Metaphorical Fugue*. New York: Vintage, 1979.

———. *I Am a Strange Loop*. New York: Basic Books, 2007.

Hughlings-Jackson, J. "On a Particular Variety of Epilepsy ('Intellectual Aura'), One Case with Symptoms of Organic Brain Disease." *Brain* 2 (1889) 179–207.

Institute of Human Origins. *Becoming Human*. Prepared by Jay Greene, Tanya Georgevich, and Maria Paulina Greene. Interactive multimedia documentary. May 2007; corrected January 2011. Online: http://www.becominghuman.org.

James, William. *The Varieties of Religious Experience: A Study in Human Nature*. 1902. Reprint, New York: Penguin, 1982.

Janik, V. M., et al. "Signature Whistle Shape Conveys Identity Information to Bottlenose Dolphins." *Proceedings of the National Academy of Sciences of the United States of America* 103 (2006) 8293–97.

Jaynes, Julian. "The Evolution of Language in the Late Pleistocene." *Annals of the New York Academy of Sciences* 280 (1976) 312–25.

———. *The Origin of Consciousness in the Breakdown of the Bicameral Mind*. 1976. Reprint, Boston: Houghton Mifflin, 1990.

Johanson, D. C., and M. Taieb. "Plio-Pleistocene Hominid Discoveries in Hadar, Ethiopia."*Nature* 260 (1976) 293–97.

Karmiloff-Smith, Annette. *Beyond Modularity: A Developmental Perspective on Cognitive Science*. Cambridge, MA: MIT Press, 1992.

Klein, Richard G., with Blake Edgar. *The Dawn of Human Culture*. New York: Wiley & Sons, 2004.

Knight, Nicola, et al. "Children's Attributions of Beliefs to Humans and God: Cross-Cultural Evidence." *Cognitive Science* 2 (2004) 117–26.

Knight, Nicola. "Yukatek Mayan Children's Attributions of Belief to Natural and Non-natural entities." *Journal of Cognition and Culture* 8 (2008) 235–43.

Kummer, Hans, and Jane Goodall. "Conditions of Innovative Behaviour in Primates." *Philosophical Transactions of the Royal Society of London* B308 (1985) 203–14.

Leakey, L. S .B., et al. "A New Species of the Genus *Homo* from Olduvai Gorge." *Nature* 202 (1964) 7–9.

Bibliography

Leakey, M. D., and R. L. Hay. "Pliocene Footprints in the Laetolil Beds at Laetoli, Northern Tanzania." *Nature* 278 (1979) 317–23.

Leakey, M. G., et al., "New Specimens and Confirmation of an Early Age for *Australopithecus Anamensis.*" *Nature* 393 (1998) 62–66.

Leavens, D., and W. Hopkins. "Intentional Communication by Chimpanzees: A Cross-Sectional Study of the Use of Referential Gestures." *Developmental Psychology* 34 (1998) 813–22.

Libet, Benjamin, et al. "Time of Conscious Intention to Act in Relation to Onset of Cerbral Activity (Rediness-Potential)." *Brain* 106 (1983) 623–42.

Loder, James. *The Transforming Moment: Understanding Convictional Experiences.* San Francisco: Harper & Row, 1981.

Loder, James E., and Jim W. Neidhardt. *The Knight's Move: The Relational Logic of the Spirit in Theology and Science.* Colorado Springs: Helmers & Howard, 1992.

Lohmann, Kenneth J., et al. "Regional Magnetic Fields as Navigational Markers for Sea Turtles." *Science* 294 (October 12, 2001) 364–66.

Lorenz, Edward. "The Butterfly Effect." Premio Felice Pietro Chisesi e Caterina Tomassoni award lecture, University of Rome, Rome, April, 2008. Online: http://eapsweb.mit.edu/research/Lorenz/Miscellaneous/Tomassoni_2008.pdf.

———. "Predictability: Does the Flap of a Butterfly's Wings in Brazil Set Off a Tornado in Texas?" Presentation to the American Association for the Advancement of Science, Section on Environmental Sciences, New Approaches to Global Weather, Boston, MA, December 29, 1972. Online: http://eapsweb.mit.edu/research/Lorenz/Butterfly_1972.pdf.

Maclean, Norman. *A River Runs Through It and Other Stories.* 1976. Reprint, New York: Pocket Books, 1992.

McDougall, Ian, et al. "Stratigraphic Placement and Age of Modern Humans from Kibish, Ethiopia." *Nature* 433 (2005) 733–36.

M. C. Escher: The Official Website. Online: http://www.mcescher.com.

Mcrearty, Sally, and Alison S. Brooks. "The Revolution That Wasn't." *Journal of Human Evolution* 39 (2000) 453–563.

Merleau-Ponty, Maurice. *Phenomenology of Perception.* Translated by Colin Smith. London: Routledge & Kegan Paul, 1962.

Mithen, Steven J. *After the Ice: A Global Human History 20,000–5,000 BC.* Cambridge, MA: Harvard University Press, 2003.

———. *The Prehistory of the Mind: A Search for the Origins of Art, Religion, and Science.* London: Thames and Hudson, 1996.

———. *The Singing Neanderthals: The Origins of Music, Language, Mind, and Body.* Cambridge, MA: Harvard University Press, 2006.

Moltmann, Jürgen. *God in Creation: A New Theology of Creation and the Spirit of God.* San Francisco: HarperCollins, 1985.

———. *The Way of Jesus Christ.* San Francisco: HarperCollins, 1990.

Moses, Louis J., and Michael J. Chandler. "Review: Traveler's Guide to Children's Theories of Mind." *Psychological Inquiry* 3 (1992) 286–301.

Nagel, Thomas. "What Is It Like to Be a bat?" *Philosophical Review* 83 (1974) 435–50.

Nagell, K., et al. "Processes of Social Learning in the Tool Use of Chimpanzees (*Pan troglodytes*) and Human Children (*Homo sapiens*)." *Journal of Comparative Psychology* 107 (1993) 174–86.

NASA. "Earth's Inconstant Magnetic Field." December 29, 2003. Online: http://www.nasa. gov/vision/earth/lookingatearth/29dec_magneticfield.html.

——. "Universe 101: Our Universe." Online: http://map.gsfc.nasa.gov/universe/uni_ age.

National Geographic. "Gelada Monkeys." Video. Online: http://video.nationalgeographic. com/video/animals/mammals-animals/monkeys-and-lemurs/baboon_gelada/.

Němec, Pavel, et al. "Neuroanatomy of Magnetoreception: The Superior Colliculus Involved in Magnetic Orientation in a Mammal." *Science* 294 (October 12, 2001) 366–68.

Nørretranders, Tor. *The User Illusion: Cutting Consciousness Down to Size.* Translated by Jonathan Sydenham. New York: Viking, 1998.

Origen. *On First Principles.* In *An Exhortation to Martyrdom, Prayer, First Principles, Book IV, Prologue to the Commentary on the Song of Songs, Homily XXVI on Numbers.* Translated by Rowan A. Greer. The Classics of Western Spirituality. New York: Paulist, 1979.

Pannenberg, Wolfhart. *Anthropology in Theological Perspective.* Translated by Matthew J. O'Connell. Philadelphia: Westminster, 1985.

Piaget, Jean. *The Child's Conception of Time.* Translated by A. J. Pomerans. 1927. Reprint, New York: Basic Books, 1969.

——. *Six Psychological Studies.* Translated by Anita Tenser and David Elkind. New York: Random House, 1967.

Piaget, Jean, and Barbel Inhelder. *The Psychology of the Child.* Translated by Helen Weaver. 1966. Reprint, New York: Basic Books, 1969.

——. *The Child's Conception of Space.* Translated by F. J. Langdon and J. L. Lunzer. Norton Library 408. New York: Norton, 1967.

Plato. *The Republic.* Translated by B. Jowett. New York: Modern Library, 1982.

Popol Vuh: The Mayan Book of the Dawn of Life. Translated by Dennis Tedlock. New York: Simon & Schuster, 1985.

Richmond, Bruce. "Rhythm and Melody in Gelada Vocal Exchanges." *Primates* 28 (1987) 199–223.

Sacks, Oliver W. *Musicophilia: Tales of Music and the Brain.* New York: Knopf, 2007.

Smithsonian Natural Museum of History. "Geologic Time: The Story of a Changing Earth." Interactive multimedia presentation. Online: http://paleobiology.si.edu/ geotime/.

Sosis, Richard. "The Adaptationist-Byproduct Debate on the Evolution of Religion: Five Misunderstandings of the Adaptationist Program." *Journal of Cognition and Culture* 9 (2009) 315–32.

Spitz, Rene. *The First Year of Life: A Psychoanalytic Study of Normal and Deviant Development of Object Relations.* New York: International Universities Press, 1965.

Swisher, C. C., and W. J. Rink. "Latest *Homo erectus* of Java: Potential Contemporaneity with *Homo sapiens* in Southeast Asia." *Science* 274 (1996) 1870–74.

Struever, Stuart, and Felicia Antonelli Holton. *Koster: Americans in Search of Their Prehistoric Past.* Prospect Heights, IL: Waveland, 1979.

Tomasello, Michael. *The Cultural Origins of Human Cognition.* Cambridge, MA: Harvard University Press, 1999

——. "How Are Humans Unique?" *New York Times Magazine,* May 25, 2008, 15.

——. *Origins of Human Communication.* Cambridge, MA: MIT Press, 2008.

Bibliography

Tomasello, Michael, et al. "The Comprehension of Novel Communicative Signs by Apes and Human Children. *Child Development* 68 (1997) 1067–81.

———. "Understanding and Sharing Intentions: The Origins of Cultural Cognition." *Behavioral and Brain Science* 28 (2005) 675–735.

Tomasello, Michael, and Josep Call. *Primate Cognition*. Oxford: Oxford University Press, 1997.

Trevena, Judy and Jeff Miller, "Brain preparation before a voluntary action: Evidence against unconscious movement initiation," *Consciousness and Cognition* 19 (2010) 447–56.

Ulanov, Ann Belford. "The Gift of Consciousness." *Princeton Seminary Bulletin*, n.s., 19 (1998) 242–58.

University of California Museum of Paleontology. "Online Exhibits." Online: http://www.ucmp.berkeley.edu/exhibits/.

U.S. Geological Survey. "Education." Online: http://education.usgs.gov.

Van Huyssteen, J. Wentzel. *Alone in the World: Human Uniqueness in Science and Theology.* Grand Rapids: Eerdmans, 2006.

Vonnegut, Kurt. *Breakfast of Champions.* New York: Dial Press, 1973.

Wellman, H., et al. "Meta-Analysis of Theory of Mind Development: The Truth about False-Belief." *Child Development,* 72 (2001) 655–84.

White, T. D., et al. "*Australopithecus ramidus,* a New Species of Early Hominid from Aramis, Ethiopia." *Nature* 371 (1994) 306–12.

Wigger, J. Bradley. "Facing the Fear of Stickiness: A Theology of Parenting." *Horizons* 12 (1999) 4–6.

———. "Phase II." *See-Through Knowing: A Site Dedicated to Invisible Friends.* Online: http://seethroughknowing.com/about/phase-ii/.

———. "See-Through Knowing: Learning from Children and Their Invisible Friends." *Journal of Childhood and Religion* 2/3 (2011). Online: http://www.childhoodandreligion.com/JCR/Volume_2_(2011)_files/Wigger%20May%202011.pdf.

———. *The Texture of Mystery: An Interdisciplinary Inquiry into Perception and Learning.* London: Associated University Presses, 1998.

Wigger, J. Bradley, et al. "What Do Invisible Friends Know?: Imaginary Companions, God, and Theory of Mind." *International Journal for the Psychology of Religion* (forthcoming).

Wong, Kate. "Rethinking the Hobbits of Indonesia." *Scientific American* 301 (2009) 66–73.

Wood, Bernard. "Paleoanthropology: Hominid Revelations from Chad." *Nature* 418 (2002) 133–35.

World Wildlife Fund. "Monarch of Migration." Online: http://www.worldwildlife.org/monarchs/.

Wray, Alison. "Protolanguage as a Holistic System for Social Interaction." *Language & Communication* 18 (1998) 47–67.

Wray, Alison, and William Grace. "The Consequences of Talking to Strangers: Evolutionary Corollaries of Socio-cultural Influences on Linguistic Form." *Lingua* 117 (2007) 543–78.

Zeman, Adam. *Consciousness: A User's Guide.* New Haven, CT: Yale University Press, 2002.